Hello, Mr. Carreras
The Story of a Personal Renaissance

Hello, Mr. Carreras
The Story of a Personal Renaissance

By

Nancy Warren

Cover design and illustration by
Rachel Hélena Barnes
All Rights Reserved, January 2,000

1stBooks-rev.3/24/00

About the Book

"Hello, Mr. Carreras" chronicles a personal experience with an overwhelming creative and spiritual inspiration as it unfolds over a period of two years in a profound series of events which completely transform the life of the author, Nancy Warren, and her entire family -- all as the result of hearing a man sing.

The cataclysmic episode begins with a public television broadcast of an opera concert which the writer, then a successful, affluent businesswomen with no particular interest in opera, coincidently overhears from an adjoining room. The voice is that of José Carreras, notably a world famous tenor, but a singer completely unknown to the listener. The encounter inexplicably triggers an avalanche of emotional and spiritual crisis, and an artistic renaissance, in her life.

Finding this overwhelming transformation incredible and frightening, yet undeniably real and exhilarating, she begins a vigorous search of the disciplines of psychology, philosophy, music, world history, quantum physics, mythology and religion for possible explanations of her reaction to this vocalist.

And, in the course of her persistent search for the facts about Carreras, as her usually orderly personal and professional existence turns upside down, she abandons her lifelong business goals and begins a career on the ground floor in opera production. In this way, she hopes to increase her knowledge of the vocalist and of the operatic Art form in order to interview Carreras, understand his impact on her life, and write about him.

As a consequence of her determined quest, this respected and wealthy business executive soon finds her future forever altered in a traumatic loss of career, marriage, home and financial security. Yet, an irresistible inspiration persistently propells her into musical and literary pursuits she had once considered beyond her grasp.

Even more amazing, the author's backstage investigation of opera as she prepares academically for a person-to-person interview with José Carreras leads to fresh discoveries about the nature and source of the Universe, an encounter with angelic forces, and a new appreciation for the creative power of music.

Dedication

This book is dedicated to my Mother, Dorothy, who first sang the music for me; and to my Father, Bob, whose love continues to sustain and inspire me, even after his passing.

Table of Contents

Preface

Yesterday something extraordinary happened. In the afternoon, as I trudged up the sidewalk of my children's elementary school to gather them and take them home, a blue paneled door flew open about twenty five yards ahead and a small figure boiled down the pavement toward me, "Look! Look! Adrienne's Mother! See what I have! I won it myself!"

Six year old Jessica, a friend of my daughter Adrienne, hurtled toward me with her hair flying, wreathed in smiles, illuminated with joy. I dropped to one knee to meet her at eye level.

A few feet away, she stopped and walked forward slowly, the slightest hint of ceremony in her gait. Then she quietly laid a small green object in my hand. It was a laminated paper cut-out of an eighth note, on its flag flew a brightly colored decal of a blue bird, singing for all it was worth.

"I won it in music," she said in a hushed voice, cupping both her hands around mine to keep the paper from blowing away, "I sang for the class." Together, we inspected her prize in silence.

I wanted to recognize the significance of this moment for her. "I'm proud of you," I said, "You know, it looks like it must be an eighth note from an especially beautiful melody."

Jessica gave me an earnest look. "Yes," she said, "it is, it's a note from my melody. And as soon as I know the rest of it, I promise, I'll come back and sing it for you."

Then, with a delicate motion of the hand, she reclaimed her award and disappeared down the sidewalk, leaving me in her debt. For now I will ever imagine that, at our birth, God tenderly places a single musical note in each of our hearts saying, "With this you can find your melody; you will know the rest when you hear it. And when you find your song, please remember I love you, and sing it for me."

Chapter One

On rare occasion, cooking pasta primavera can be a memorable experience. For instance, on an evening when the primavera never makes it into the pan, when pasta preparation is halted by a life-altering event. I've noticed it's the peeling of the garlic that always takes longest. I suppose when God invented them, so tiny and tightly clothed, he didn't take into account that you would need forty cloves to make a decent sauce. And for that I must be grateful. Because, in this instance, if I had not left my gardening early to peel garlic, if I had not been hanging over the garbage disposal for half an hour skinning and crushing these smelly little vegetables, I never would have heard the song in the first place. "Il lamento de Federico," I mean. Like most better known lamentos, it's the story of lost love and grief and the wish for peace of mind. Something all mothers can relate to.

In theory at least, I have pulled the dials off our television so that, as far as the children are concerned, we receive only a single channel, the Public Broadcasting System. And, without the ability to tune in to "Under Dog," my daughter and son, ages four and six, were relieved to see the end of the "McNeil/Lehrer Report" and had jacked up the volume on an operatic concert. The children understand this madness, the theoretical lack of dials, although they'd probably settle for "Ren and Stimpy" cartoons if they could.

They're willing to live with my version of reality, however, because I've made a career of pointing out to them how they feel, how they talk, how they behave -- to saying nothing of how I feel, talk and behave -- when they watch mindless entertainment. And this in contrast to how uplifted and inspired they become when they watch something worthwhile. So the sound of an operatic aria wafting forth between the outbreaks of arm wrestling and giggles in the family room did not surprise me. The voice with which it was delivered did.

The first notes passed my ear and rolled around the kitchen, tantalizing. Who was that singing? Oh, I'll think of the name. Let's see, that must be... It was a voice I recognized from

1

somewhere far in the past. In fact, the recognition was so absolute, I felt I knew the pain inside the words by heart although the song was unfamiliar. Now, this is silly. Don't you hate it when a name, a face, flirts at the edge of your mind and refuses to be identified? Now think, the name sounds like...it rhymes with... I drew a blank.

"Who's singing, kids?" I called into the other room.

"Some guy," they answered. Wonderful. For this I sent them to all the best schools.

Overcome with curiosity, I set my garlic mountain aside, grabbed a blue checked tea towel to wipe my hands and rounded the corner into the family room, still talking.

"I know who it is, I'd know that voice anywhere. I just can't think of the name," I babbled.

Somewhere along the line, we had thought it important to invest in a projection television with a screen approximately the size of a bed sheet. All of this for one channel and the screening of a few videos. Talk about schizophrenia. But despite this enormous visual aid, I could not identify the singer. In fact, I found myself gazing at a gentleman I had never seen in my life; a friendly looking man in formal concert attire, with black wavy hair and sparkling dark eyes. He finished his song with appreciative gestures to the audience and conductor. Typical of PBS and its love of the cognescenti, I thought, that nothing indicated who the artist was as he bowed, waved and disappeared from the stage, unidentified.

Being denied the facts enflames the imagination of a certain type of person who cannot do without knowing. Once the red flag, the incendiary of inquisitiveness, has been waved before this variety of animal, thunder will roll, life will cease and Hell will be declared on earth until the question, whatever it may be, is answered. I am such a monster. Dinner went on hold as we sat breathlessly before the television, waiting for this person to appear once more. Had I imagined the familiar quality of his voice? Why could I not recognize who this was? And what would I do with all that garlic now that the kids had ordered pizza?

Tenors Luciano Pavarotti and Placido Domingo did the honors for the next four pieces. The singer in question did not reappear for some time; not until nearly the middle of the program. Then, again unidentified, he sang "Core 'Ngrato":

"Catari, Catari, perche me dici sti parole amare?" [Catherine, Catherine, why do you address me only with bitter words?]

Curiosity turned to fascination. And as the song continued, an awareness descended, the cognizance of a transcendent quality which glowed about this man. His performance shone with intensity, discipline, serenity and presence, with the grace of an archangel unfolding luminous wings. He sang straight from his soul. I was in awe.

"Mama, the pizza man's here!" My son, Daniel, danced in front of me. In semi-trance, I grabbed my purse from beside the sofa and handed him my wallet, vaguely hoping he would not tip the delivery boy more than fifty dollars or so. The children quickly set up dinner trays and began grazing on the extra cheese and pepperonis, watching me keenly with huge, brown eyes.

They have learned to cope with having a writer for a mother --have suffered through the production of everything from public relations brochures and poetry to a novel -- and can actively follow the various stages of my creative delirium. A startling fact, a play on words, or any sudden inspiration roils its way into an emotional preoccupation, then a poem, a chapter, a short story. And the urgency of identifying this singer and knowing more about him had escalated to the potential of a five alarm emotional emergency. No one spoke for the rest of the program as I concentrated.

Domingo and Pavarotti came and went on the screen. I had admired both of them over the years and collected some of their musical recordings. But it was this other vocalist who now had my undivided attention as he rolled out the "R's" in the song "Granada," with evident patriotism and perfect pronunciation. He must be a Spaniard, I decided. Toward the end of the program, he sang once more alone. An aria I recognized from Giordano's opera "Andrea Chenier,"

"One day I stood raptly gazing
at the blue vault of heaven
and at the flower-filled meadows;
the sun rained showers of gold
and the earth was a golden splendour;
the world seemed a limitless treasure,
and the firmament its casket.
The earth breathed a caress,
a living kiss upon my face.
Completely overcome by love, I cried:
I love you, you who kiss my face, my
heavenly beautiful motherland."

With this song the crisis deepened in dimension. Some different emotion took over. "Mama's crying," Daniel whispered to his sister, who between gulps of milk tossed a handful of kleenex to me from the box on the coffee table. First just Daniel, then both children, watched with astonishment and concern as I struggled for control. This was a new one on them.

"Are you alright, Mama?," they wanted to know. I was not, although I nodded affirmatively for their benefit. I had been hit head-on by a consuming and indefinable sort of comprehension; something of the magnitude of being struck by lightning. I had the sense of watching an old friend, someone I had not heard from in a great while and missed; the overwhelming feeling that I not only knew this person who sang, but had something important to discuss with him or he with me. Ridiculous. No, asinine would be a better word. How would we communicate? We probably couldn't speak even one of the same languages fluently. And, anyway, why would I have that impression of someone I had never even heard of before? I did not know so much as his name. It was a baffling and disconcerting occurrence. I could not decide whether to be intrigued, frightened, or just plain annoyed. Whatever was happening was completely unique in my experience and beyond logical explanation.

The three tenors rallied on stage for a medley of folk songs, Broadway tunes, and other odds and ends. They closed with an encore of the aria "Nessun Dorma" which brought the audience to its feet. Finally, at the end of forever, the credits ran. I followed intently as they scrolled up the screen.

"Well, at long last, at least you have a name," I said. "Hello, Mr. Carreras."

Chapter Two

There's nothing quite so offensive to a librarian as sticky hands and a loud mouth. Children generally have both and this might be the only reason I had not just moved us and our belongings into the University of Arizona library immediately following the now-famous three tenors', "Carreras, Domingo, Pavarotti," concert at Caracalla. I had expected the strange emotion which had seized me to disappear by the next morning; thought I would be able to dismiss it all as a mistake. A fluke. My imagination. Overexposure to garlic juice. But the following day, nothing had changed.

The intense feeling that I had witnessed something remarkable in Carreras' performance persisted and haunted me. What on earth was I to do with this odd emotion? I had the eerie feeling that the earth had shaken under my feet, that no day would ever look exactly ordinary again. Did things like this happen to people who are just innocently cooking spaghetti, minding their own business? And if so, why? Was it possible anyone else had had this experience and bothered to document it? Completely baffled, but hopeful, my only instinct was to try to make something productive of this unusual event, to head for the library and spend whatever time was required to figure out my problem.

Maybe it was connected with the music, I thought. Music had been an important part of my life since childhood, although I had never before gotten quite so overwrought about it. My Mother is an artist and encouraged all of us in the Arts from an early age. My brother, sister and I each played several musical instruments, sang and performed in music theater. Initially, I had started begging for a piano and a book of Chopin at the age of four and the family assumed I'd become a concert pianist like Mother's Grandfather, Edgar Shaftoe Lovel. He was a paragon who had left England, abandoning his interest in a British peerage, just to become an American concert performer. But,

7

without the virtue of his single-mindedness, I soon widened my interests to include French horn, violin, guitar and, of course, voice.

To our family, singing seemed a natural extension of being alive, since Mother had a prolific memory for music and serenaded all of us and the world in general from dawn to dusk. You knew what time she got out of bed, because you heard her song. Nearly every night I fell asleep to the sound of her voice. Music was often the center of our entertainment and memories of home, as most family events and holidays ended with us and our guests around the piano, Mother's sheet music piled up everywhere and all of us warbling away. At our house, to ask "Do you like to sing?" would be equivalent to asking "Do you like to breathe?"

Besides Mother's influence, since we lived on the East Coast conveniently situated between Philadelphia and New York City, we took our inspiration from Broadway musical theater, opera and concerts of all varieties, particularly from events at the Academy of Music, where we spent many Wednesday nights of the student concert season seated at the feet of Eugene Ormandy and the Philadelphia orchestra. Yet, just a dozen feet away from this legendary conductor and his countless prominent guest soloists, I had never empathized so thoroughly with any musical interpretation as with that of Mr. Carreras. Who was he? What had I heard? What did it mean? When stumped by life, I head for the largest collection of books available.

Within a few days I knew more about Mr. Carreras. He was a native Catalan, born in Barcelona, Spain. His given name "Josep" was generally translated from the Catalan into Spanish: "José." And that was how he was known around the world, as José Carreras. Music critics thought highly of Mr. Carreras. He was an accomplished vocal artist who had sung in all the major operatic theatres of the world. "A meteoric career," they said in several different languages.

I had loved opera since the age of fourteen when I heard music playing in the record department of Hess Brother's' store in Allentown, Pennsylvania; the most beautiful music imaginable. While everyone else spent the afternoon shopping, I sat by a stereo display and the salesman kindly played the entire album for me; a recording of Leontyne Price, Richard Tucker, Rosalind Elias and Phillip Maero singing "Madama Butterfly." The album was all I asked for for Christmas.

Later that year, friends took me to see "Cosi fan Tutti" in Philadelphia. It was a revelation. Opera could be, not only dramatically tragic, but complexly comic! The costumes, scenery, and live voices were unforgettable. In my mind, I relived it again and again. I became a fan of this intricate musical art and fell completely out of sync with most of my contemporaries. To me, in comparison with opera and the thrill of live performance, the television was just a piece of furniture.

Although I hardly considered myself a connoisseur of opera, it seemed impossible that I had neither heard a Carreras recording or any news of his celebrated career in the ensuing years. Perhaps it was because, despite Carreras' fame, the readily available literature about him was limited, consisting of reviews and a couple magazine articles. And after a week of searching, I still had no real concept of the man's background, or any remote explanation for my reaction to his music.

I had solved very little. Even worse, I had accumulated about fifty additional questions. Simple questions. Mostly about the nature of Art, music, God and the universe. Let's see here, I deliberated, I'll check out a few books about the Big Bang, Saint Thomas Aquinas, music composition, Aristotle, physical reality. Oh yes, this was getting clearer all the time. I was confident that, within a few days, it would all work its way around and I would have identified what was gnawing inside. But weeks went by and the armful of books grew to a deskfull. The all-powerful kernel of a thought had taken over and there would be no turning back from a journey to the beginnings and ends of time, if that's what it took.

And it did. For me, comprehending a vocal performance which leaves such a profound and inexplicable imprint meant vaulting past the details of a single vocalist's life into an investigation of the fundamental nature of music; an investigation that leads from the beginnings of the cosmos to the discovery of particle physics.

I learned that, in ancient times, people built their faith around the nature of rhythm and tonal quality, living in harmony with the overarching hum of the Universe. Even without the genius and education of a single Stephen Hawkings, early homo sapiens apparently had gazed out into the blackness of the night and into their own hearts and sensed the resonance of inner and outer space, the force which stands at the center of creation: musical sound. They recognized that music has a profound effect on human beings because it contains an ultimate life-confirming power.

A shocking thought perhaps but, in essence, we are a creation of music. Our existence relies upon the ongoing agreement of some divine conscience that matter and energy in a state of musical vibration will form a physical reality, the basis for human life and all we survey. Quite literally, from those divinely generated waves of sound which form the cosmos, emanate the notes of physical existence, the music of the spheres. Forget about the sound of one hand clapping. Consider instead the reverberating waves, the resonant tremor, the sonar glue that holds this place and everything in it together. In essence, all of creation results from one grand musical score. Only God could envision such a simple, esoteric, ingenious and completely elegant design.

In a sophisticated and somewhat superfluous way, physicists, through the theorems of quantum and particle physics eventually corroborated God's behavior as a scientific probability. I say probability having learned that scientific "facts" do not actually exist. At the baseline, we can only establish what our limited senses will allow by eliminating what would appear to be all the other choices. We derive an assumption, not an absolute definition.

For example, if we observe and agree that matter and energy in a state of vibration create physical reality, we still have no idea what energy is or where it comes from. And, in the end, scientists operate as much on trust and belief as anyone.

At that rate, the supposed conflict of science and religion dissolves; its existence becomes more a matter of skewed perspectives, the conflict of two different generations of philosopher (those of faith and those of process) confronting one another, arguing from two different pools of thought and knowledge, two different intellectual eras in the history of man. What a waste of time when any halfway sensible scientist can not sleep at night without a profound spiritual understanding, any more than a religious mystic can in fact meld with some universal force and opt out of physical existence in a puff of smoke.

A clear thinker in the practical as well as the scientific world, Albert Einstein had pinpointed the nature of the conflict and its irony,

> Now, even though the realism of religion and science in themselves are clearly marked off from each other, nevertheless there exist between the two strong reciprocal relationships and dependencies. Though religion may be that which determines the goal, it has, nevertheless, learned from science in the broadest sense, what means will contribute to the attainment of the goals it has set up. But science can only be created by those who are thoroughly imbued with the aspiration towards truth and understanding... I cannot conceive of a genuine scientist without that profound faith.
>
> The situation may be expressed by an image: Science without religion is lame, religion without science is blind.

German musician and physicist, Joachim-Ernst Berendt, clearly established the connections and relationships among music, science and the spirit in his milestone work, "Nada Brahma." According to his explanation, all major religions, East and West, point to "the Word," the prime material with which God created this universe. The Word, Berendt equated with resonance, with sound. Scientists are finding that this is literally so, that creation began in some instantaneous and mystical fashion with a spontaneous vibration which has never ceased.

The sounds produced by these vibrations, physicists have identified as rhythmic, tonal, and harmonic: as music. And these vibrations are echoed, are all-pervasive throughout the natural, physical world. We now know that quarks sing, electrons hum, that hyperspace, far from expanding into endless silence hisses, calls, moans, beats, howls and roars into the limits of the cosmos.

At a speed exceeding 600,000 billion vibrations per second, waves of sound become the light, the color and substance which we perceive as our physical world. In other words, creation begins as vibration or music, translates into waves of sound, becomes light, and ultimately manifests itself within the material or physical substance of our world. All of this transpires at such speed and so mysteriously that, even at a subatomic level, physicists cannot distinguish a wave from a particle. These phenomena overlap one another.

With the advanced electronic technology of radio telescopy scientists have made previously undetected ranges of sound audible and we may listen to the tones "sung" by the nine planets. The six which are visible to us sing within the usual eight octave range of overtones and undertones easily perceived by human beings. Earth and Venus, for example, vibrate along the "G" clef, in harmony, a musical third away from each other. The three planets we cannot see, Neptune, Uranus and Pluto, hum in octaves below the range of human perception, but with a resonance that is experienced by human beings as a rhythm, a beat, the sub-woofers or bass notes of our solar system.

Back on earth, with the help of a hypersensitive listening device known as the photo-acoustic spectrograph which allows scientists to make cell growth audible, we can hear a rose blooming to its own ecstatic accompaniment, which Berendt describes as "an organ-like droning, reminiscent of the sounds of a Bach toccata or Messiaen's 'Asension' for organ--in other words, reminiscent of what in traditional organ music is perceived as a 'spread' succession of chords." Likewise, wheat waves in cadence with a self-generated golden symphonic chorus, high above our range of hearing, undetected.

From what does all this sonic upheaval emanate? First, looking for an answer among subatomic particles -- electrons, positrons and neutrons -- gazing into the internal spaces of these miniscule units of energy, scientists have discovered a highly cooperative society in which electrons must communicate either sonically or telepathically since they seem to "know," not only that they have choices to make in their behavior, but that they must anticipate the other electrons' motion before they vacate an atomic shell or bond with another element. Searching for the source of this "intelligence," and for the means of mysterious ceaseless musical sound, science has probed the inner sanctum, the internal workings of these tiny particles and found the contents astonishing: nothing, absolutely nothing.

What physicists find baffling, Hindus and Buddhists have always known about the nature of God. "Everything is nothing; nothing is everything," they have claimed for thousands of years. And in their orientation to the world and its truths; God's Word, sound, music, communication, language and vibration are one and the same, literally even the same word. Their concepts of chanting mantras and koans (repetitive Zen meditations on the unsolvable) encourage human beings to a state of universal harmony, to become One with a primal, universal sound.

I had always considered a personal mantra a spooky concept, taken up as a spiritual status symbol by neurotic Californians who had nothing better to do than hum while getting a sun tan. I developed a new respect. The mantra constitutes a communications band on the universal radio waves, and a means of becoming a competent player in the cosmic symphony. As Sufi master, Hazrat Inayat Khan, proposed in his famous treatise on music as the basis of creation [a philosophic gem which has been passed as a gift from one professional musician to another over several decades] --

"The knower of the mystery of sound knows the mystery of the whole Universe...The music of the universe is the background of the small picture which we call music. Our sense of music, our attraction to music, shows that there is music in the depth of our being. Music is behind the working of the whole universe. Music is not only life's greatest object, but is life itself."

In all of this, for many religions, the prospect of being "made in God's image" takes on serious new implications when God's creative ideal would seem to be that, even at a subatomic level, particles live cooperatively, in rhythm and harmony with everything around them; without aggression in a spirit of pure communication; when the cosmos revolves around unity and oneness with complementary tones and chords of an omnipresent, glorious symphonic score. And certainly, the apparent magical emptiness at the core of our Universe may come as a mighty shock to humanity in general, to us creatures who devote 80% of our waking energy to seeing, to recognizing a surface, two or three coordinates and therefore believing we have a definition, an understanding. It becomes ever more apparent that we do not. In our frenetic levels of activity and grasping for the "big picture," we neglect our musical senses and sensibility.

It occurred to me that we will have to cease this frenzy, close our eyes, and be still if we are ever to realize firsthand the power of our own instinct: the strength in simply listening, in listening simply. Otherwise, we remain oblivious to our musical roots, the peace and calm which stands at the center of our being; unnecessarily at sea within ourselves and in our earthly environment. We are like the man frantically searching for his glasses when they are right on his face; like one who starves unaware of the gold coins in his pocket.

Thousands of years ago, people in their innocence probably recognized their inner musical intelligence, not out of any particular wisdom or higher consciousness, but because they had the advantage of living in close connection with the earth and with their own nature. No alarm clocks told them when to get up, no sirens sounded, tea kettles whistled, horns blasted, saws whined, televisions blared, engines roared or telephones rang off the hook. Ancient man could probably hear the atoms serenading one another -- in the invisible night wind, in a cascading waterfall or the crackling of a fire -- and related the sounds of the universe to the harmonies of life.

How pitiful that with all the layers of motion and commotion we confront in our lives, despite all that we supposedly know, we now most often look on music more as a decoration to our routine, not a central touchstone of our being. This most beautiful gift serves only as a background to something more vital, more important in a schedule of endless activity. Activities like driving the car, shopping, visiting the dentist or riding in an elevator; the perpetual gathering, fixing, pushing and competing of the Twentieth Century lifestyle. It would seem time we questioned this relentless, cacophonous tyranny over our own better nature and instincts.

In contrast, the Chinese government of three or four thousand years ago, made music the source of its civilizing influence, relying upon a practice of tuning musical instruments at each provincial court to a common pitch to maintain harmony in the land. Legend says that the success of this approach relied upon the ability of the elders to identify the correct pitch for their times and conditions. The twelve-toned scale and the rhythms of life were sacred. So serious was this musical convention that rulers who through neglect or willfulness allowed their musicians to fall out of pitch were construed to be troubled or plotting insurrection.

The first Chinese emperor, Fu Hsi, is credited with the developing the definition and style of tonal art somewhere around 2800 B.C., as well as with the authorship of the initial eight hexagrams of the Book of Wisdom, the "I Ching." Fu Hsi advertised music as a force which would establish the basis for their culture and which would precipitate physical events and conditions helpful to society. The tonal arts became the foundation of a civilization which endured 5,000 years. In the course of a natural disaster or political crisis the Emperor Fu Hsi, called, not on government advisors, but on one or two of his 500 piece orchestras with instructions to set up a benevolent vibration which would resolve the problem! Fu Hsi believed that life on earth must reflect life Above and referred to music as the "all pervading influence."

Similar legends and beliefs exist in our own culture. But, how many of us even remember that Joshua brought down the

15

walls of Jericho with singing and blasts from a trumpet; or are aware of the three legendary choirs of Glastonbury in England which were credited with uniting the country and whose saintly voices were reported to halt war and famine in the land? One can only imagine how improbable and hopeless this sounds to those who today vest their hopes for humanity in laws and in politics. And yet, when's the last time any of us cried in empathy with a beautiful law or lovely political decision? In fact, how can people so noisy and dead to themselves as most of us tend to be comprehend ancient religions which set a standard, not just for purity of heart, but for purity of pitch?

It struck me what an opportunity we have at this moment in history to empower our world with an irresistible force, to illuminate the darkness with an unquenchable light! Within each of us, in every cell of our body, resides a power more accessible than that of nuclear energy, the thread which unites and connects our entire species. We need not wait to split atoms or anything else, we require no sanctions of government, any new treaty, or the construction of yet another machine. This is an innate gift and a power so strong that I was compelled to trace its existence because one day, completely unexpectedly and without realizing its source, I had felt the essence of this human power catapulted into my home through the television set.

Through recognition of this inner strength and connectedness, I realized that we have a unique opportunity in front of us to establish a new level of conversation on Earth, a joyous and magical conversation that suits our higher nature as the most successful and refined beings of Creation. We are creatures of melody, of harmony, of unity, of music; one gigantic choir that is mankind.

Intellectual hero and Professor of Literature at Sarah Lawrence College, Joseph Campbell admirably explained this state of affairs in his book, "Myths to Live By," when he noted,

> We are the children of this beautiful planet
> that we have seen photographed from the moon.
> We were not delivered into it by some god, but
> have come forth from it. We are its eyes and

mind, its seeing and thinking. And the earth, together with its sun, this light around which it flies like a moth, came forth, we are told, from a nebula; and that nebula, in turn, from space. So that we are the mind, ultimately, of space. No wonder then if its laws and ours are the same! Likewise, our depths are the depths of space, from whence all those gods sprang that men's minds in the past projected onto animals and plants, onto hills and streams, the planets in their courses, and their own peculiar social observances. Our mythology now, therefore, is to be of infinite space and its light, which is without as well as within. Like moths, we are caught in the spell of its allure, flying to it outward, to the moon and beyond and flying to it also inward. On our planet itself all dividing horizons have been shattered. We can no longer hold our loves at home and project our aggression elsewhere; for on this spaceship Earth there is no "elsewhere" any more.

And no mythology that continues to speak or to teach of "elsewhere" and "outsiders" meets the requirements of this hour.

When we acknowledge our shared musical substance, the musical score which unites us, we recognize mankind as an internally communicating and breathing organism with a common purpose. We are the electrons swirling inside the atom. What sensors will we develop to anticipate one another? Recognition of the eternal music which conntects us, of our phenomenal musical sensitivity could bridge our differences, serve our needs to cooperate, heal old wounds. With this realization, a creative flame began to burn within me. I could not have been happier to discover a gold mine in the back yard. But how does one translate elation into action?

This is a tall order. We are all reminded day in and out of the gigantic investment we have made in a scientific, technological and mechanistic culture. We are, most of us, completely entangled and willingly limit ourselves to this definition of civilization, to a regimentation of supposed "facts" without which we cannot operate, outside of which we cannot function. Our values and educational system teach children from the start the prescribed dramas which will be played out on the social, political and industrial stage. We encourage youth not to question our huge, tentacled money-making machine fueled by advertising and the media, or the examples of generals, politicians and business moguls we place before them as the primary heroes of our way of life. What qualities do their examples encourage in our children? Through these examples, what do we offer children as a definition of success, except that it somehow constitutes an ability to dominate and to rule? This falls far short of the mark when what children, what all of us, need so desperately is self-knowledge and the ability to work cooperatively.

Human life must become, not just a material, practical or physical endeavor, but the Art that it deserves to be. And, in order to set our sights on such a goal, we must alter our concept of a hero; adopt a new type of hero. We need to aspire to a different kind of mutually beneficial and cooperative consciousness. For, it has been my experience that you become like those you admire, those you stand next to and measure yourself against: physically, psychologically and emotionally. A concept which echoes Nature's principle of entrainment, that rhythm follows rhythm, that everything tends toward harmony with everything else, that organisms vibrate in sympathy with those nearest them and that, in fact, following the natural laws of entrainment, two clocks hanging together on a wall gradually will synchronize their pendulums to match each other stroke for stroke. And people follow the rhythm and tempo of other people, in keeping with their natural hunger to know and relate themselves to all things in the Universe distinct from themselves. Children in particular need to follow someone who is the best of what they can potentially be, someone who has managed to live out the highest nature that is in them.

For that reason, we must look to those who elevate their profession to the moral and qualitative level of Art, to our leaders in creativity -- the interpreters, translators, and instructors of our civilization -- as heroes. For it is the Arts which unite us, which transcend the limitations of verbal languages, which minimize the differences between us and capitalize upon our common understandings of life. And, similarly, we must all of us become participants in the independent investigation and understanding of our real nature as a human species, as organisms connected in every possible way with everything else in the Universe.

I was encouraged to think I had been led to this conclusion because I had already witnessed the performance of someone who would understand all of this, someone who served meritoriously as a living example of its truth. Was that perhaps the nature of the discussion I had felt I needed to have with him? And, if so, what purpose would it serve? If we agreed on all points, where would that lead? Nothing seemed clear. Yet, my belief persisted that my instincts were valid, that they mattered.

It was in searching for substance to support that belief that I soon knew most of what was in print about José Carreras. It surprised me to learn that he had recently recovered from life-threatening leukemia and had been the subject of great media attention. I tried to think where I had been to have missed this eloquently publicized, poignant drama. Especially since everyone I asked said they had read or heard about Carreras' illness when it occurred. Everyone but me. But then, for three years around that time I had been collaborating on a novel.

"No wonder. The world stops, Mom, when you're writing," admonished my eldest, Rachel, a quick and perceptive adolescent who calls a dullard a dullard. "Of course you didn't know. When you're working, you don't know what planet this is." Why not, I could accept this as a rational excuse for social paralysis. Still, from all accounts, most of the world with the exception of me, had had the presence of mind to send a get well card at the least.

"I'm sure he didn't notice," my daughter assured me.

I scanned every database for a biography of Carreras. There had to be much more to this man than critical reviews and news of his recovery. But the card catalogue offered nothing. When "Decca" Records released the video tape of the Caraccala concert I quickly seized my only opportunity to try to come to grips with who this person was; this individual who, by then, had inspired me to read half the nonfiction in the university library, delving into subjects I would have ordinarily considered far outside my interest.

For three days, the tape ran incessantly. First just to hear the songs and all the fun of the concert again. Then to try to be analytical. What was in the voice, the gestures, his rapport with the orchestra, the audience or the other performers? Why wasn't the nature of the magic more apparent, even for magic? I focused intently for a clue.

"Are you going to write about him, Mama?," my little one, Adrienne asked.

So often I find young children read your thoughts. For I had just been wondering why no Carreras biography existed. Somebody should write about a heroic performer that sings with everything in his soul. Could it be me?

Actually, I wasn't sure what to do with these new emotions and information. And the uneasy feeling was gathering that I was missing some important facts. That the other shoe was about to drop. No, something even stronger. That the earth underfoot was still trembling. That more drastic events were to come. That on the peaks above our heads, an avalanche had begun.

Chapter Three

As we grow from childhood to maturity, how do we lose the abilities we had to imbue life with excitement? Why do we develop a preference for sameness and predictability; relinquish those dreams and qualities which made us individual and unique? From all indications, the need for security far outlives curiosity in most of us. Innocence gradually dies, at the hands of what we would like to call practicality, or even necessity. Really, I believe the culprit is fear. The fear of being different, alone, unappreciated, unsuccessful, of risk and rejection, of scorn and the displeasure of others. These are the villains who kill our sense of wonder.

Fortunately, with practice, we can revive the magic. We need not look far for examples of what it was all about. I vividly remember a day in my daughter's first grade class when I observed twenty children in the midst of learning about buoyancy and flotation. Each child had brought a number of objects from home and was guessing whether their articles would sink or float, then testing them in a pan of water. Well, you know how it is with little kids and water. A whole contingent immediately needed to run to the bathroom. They tore down the hallway and back, panicked that they would miss any of the fun of the discovery. Two little girls, in their haste, returned with their dresses tucked into their underwear. Without missing a moment, they were right back into the fray, immediately focused on the excitement at hand, wearing their underwear on the outside. How incredibly wonderful that, not only did they not recognize their grave faux pas, nobody else cared either!

This, to me, represents life as Art. I am not suggesting that we all start dressing with some bizarre fashion sense. I am suggesting that we drop the self conscious poses, the supposed practical necessities, long enough to allow life to be extraordinary, to be amazing. For it is only when we view our experience with this kind of wholeness, focus, intensity, that we can begin to transcend the ordinary. We are all artists, creators of our own destiny. Artists who have learned to ignore inspiration when it sits at our feet and stares us in the face. We need to relearn how to be in the moment, rather than beside it or ahead of it as our preoccupation with the details of life, our purported maturity and responsibility, teach us to be. Because every one of us has something important to contribute, something critical to say.

From living in the moment, being fully aware of the opportunities life offers, at the instant they are offered, we can begin to develop a sense of this "something," of our true purpose in being. Then the inspiration to address that purpose, to create, will start to challenge us, to question the way we live, the way we limit ourselves. That inspiration will push and bully us until we have torn away from the imaginary shackles that prevent us from aspiring to the best in ourselves.

And, no doubt about it, that is a frightening experience. I know because now I too have had to face it. The night I heard Carreras sing began an avalanche that gradually rearranged the landscape of the rest of my life. I don't know how or why, only that it is so. At first, the nature of this inspiration was unclear and I certainly gave it insufficient credit for its tenacity. After my initial reaction to Carreras' singing, I had expected this emotional power to recede, that everything would go dutifully back into its place, then I hoped that it would, and finally in frustration commanded that it should. But this force would not be ordered to heel, would not retreat in favor of something more usual, more acceptable to my sense of order, propriety and normalcy.

It became necessary to try to understand and accept how to live with what I began to refer to mentally as The Uninvited Guest. Since the night this feeling, this awareness, this power, blew in the door on the melody of Carreras' song, I have tried in every way to analyze and understand it, to pin it down and define it. The Uninvited Guest resists analysis. With no clear idea of what to do otherwise, I politely requested that it leave. But I had let it in too far already. The Uninvited Guest not only would not

22

depart, but followed me everywhere, quietly but with laser-like precision pointing out the deficient parts of my life.

"See here," said The Guest, "You fool yourself. What is this indecision here, the phoniness and half-heartedness there? You expend so much energy and accomplish little that interests you. You mistake guilt and habit for necessity; money for happiness. You cheat yourself and everyone else, trading convenience for passion. Look at this compromise, and this and that one!"

When The Guest lingered on and on, I decided this must have significance beyond what I had originally surmised. Maybe I HAD to write a book about Carreras or this thing would never leave me in peace. Should I write to this man? Should I call him on the phone? And if I reached him, how would I explain? "Hello, Mr. Carreras, you don't know me but your friend here is driving me crazy and trashing my life." That would sound impressive.

Intermittently, out of sheer frustration, I decided to give The Guest the old heave-ho. I would demand it's exit from the premises. "OK.," I would say with conviction, "Thanks for all the great criticism and your unsolicited opinions. Thanks for making me doubt everything about myself. Now get out!"

And, at each such juncture, some person or some message would magically appear to caution me. "No, listen. Listen just a little longer."

Now, The Guest lives here, unchallenged. Dispassionately, irreverently, turning my life upside down, reordering my existence. It has become a matter of faith that all will turn out well. As the epitome of ambivalence, I inch forward. For how is it that under the influence of this inspiration, this bully, bit by bit, my life begins to feel like one which belongs to me, one in which I am not just an observer but the creative force? I, who had everything and was miserable, begin to sense the goal, the something: a shelter of inspiration, the excitement of creativity, a feeling of destiny, the comfort of finally arriving where I belong, the joy of living in the moment. Is it some unseen miracle? And, if so, where did it come from?

All I am sure of is that everything I had known is gone, blown away and out of sight. And, this uninvited inspiration pushed me out of complacency, out of a lifestyle that to most appeared privileged and perfect, but which was gradually turning my spirit to dust.

To explain, we need some history here. To be precise, I had worked for fifteen years in varied facets of business, a career I had fallen into as a matter of convenience and financial security, that came as the result of my husband accepting a position in Arizona helping to found a new human services organization for troubled adolescents. Eventually, he became very successful, established as Executive Vice President and a primary stockholder of what was to be a huge national corporation with a subsidiary video production company and a retail clothing division.

Although initially I was just along for the ride, the Chairman of the Board soon asked me to work as his personal troubleshooter. An unexpected request, since I had no business experience to speak of. I grew up in Bucks County, Pennsylvania, in a community of gentleman farmers; majored at school in literature and languages; worked throughout college as a clothing model, a public relations writer and as an interpreter for an international company's bilingual board meetings, then married young. I knew virtually nothing of business, but decided to try the position offered because my husband was so completely consumed by work that business meetings might be the only opportunity I would have to see him.

Over fifteen years, my boss and I communicated almost entirely by telephone. I rarely saw him in person and rarely needed to. Our styles complemented one another since I worked best on my own and he had little time to supervise. He was the harried leader of a large company and had slim tolerance for discussion. He was dyslexic and unable to read complicated business reports, relying upon me to research and define problems, then recommend what to do about them. In general our conversations ended with him telling me, "Well go fix it."

As a result of this unique relationship, I started a new career creating entirely new business ventures every couple years in the varied positions of head of management information systems, director of purchasing, fleet manager, chief of contract negotiations, risk manager, public relations executive, and on and on. I learned object-oriented systems engineering in order to design and install a multi-million dollar computer system and build custom software. As a writer, I produced video scripts, speeches and public relations material for the subsidiary video production company; worked with CBS, NBC and the BBC on documentary productions about the program's success with troubled children, and co-authored a nonfiction novel about my boss's life as a human services entrepreneur.

Overall, I found that I was a complete misfit in the corporate mold, among a domineering contingent of hostilely aggressive, competitive males who listened to me solely because I was the only one who had read the instructions. After a time, I believe I openly yawned at their metaphors which explained literally every human experience in terms of a famous football strategy.

In general, there was no explanation for my survival in the corporate world, except that, as Mark Twain once said, "Nothing succeeds like ignorance and confidence." It sounded like my job qualifications. Absolute naivete and lack of preconceived notions probably helped in that I hadn't the sense to be intimidated by the competition, the magnitude of the problems, or vast sets of new skills which I had to acquire.

At the close of each mini-career I faced the same question, "Would you like to stay on and run this department?" I never stayed. Once the creative process was complete, the new business department in motion, I had lost interest and lit out with my rope and pick, looking for the next mountain peak. I couldn't imagine driving to the same office each day, facing repetitive problems. Nothing in business had an enduringly inspiring quality; nothing fit over the long term.

Yet, I remained, lulled by all the diverse opportunity that masqueraded as success, finding the process of overcoming endless hurdles momentarily interesting but oddly unfulfilling. No, I didn't want to endlessly supervise anything. And, with that decision came the increasing risk that there might not be a next mountain, that if I succeeded in solving the company's growth problems, I might be out of a job. Professionally, I was painting my way into a corner.

One momentous day, things got worse. I know almost the exact date and time I became a compulsive workaholic. At first, we had been told we were expecting twins. Four months later, on a tragic November morning, the fetal heartbeats had stopped, I was hemorrhaging and being rushed into emergency surgery. When I awoke in a hospital room, the surgeon was sitting alone with me, holding my hand. He looked grave.

"You have a rare type of cancer that stems from pregnancy," he said. "I'm so sorry."

He explained that he thought he had removed the tumor, but that the assurance of a cure was two years away. Any recurrence would advance rapidly, so I would need to undergo a series of tests every four weeks. He also cautioned that any new pregnancy within the next eighteen months certainly would prove fatal. For me, the news was dire, uninmaginable. If I died, who would raise my young daughter, Rachel? For my husband, the scenario was overwhelming and beyond tolerance.

"I can't stand it," he said. "Go ahead and cry and then I never want to hear about it again."

During the months of testing and evaluation he couldn't bring himself to acknowledge the diagnosis, was oblivious to the endless schedule of doctor's appointments and constant waiting for results. The prediction that I would die from a future pregnancy was absurd in his view. He simply refused to accept any change in the status quo.

Desperate with terror and loneliness, I at first focused entirely on managing and understanding every aspect of the medical therapy myself. Abandoned in the struggle, I soon realized that sharing the diagnosis with family and friends was my choice. After careful consideration, I told no one. The extreme nature of the disease would not be obvious since chemotherapy was useless. My parents lived three thousand miles away and there seemed no point in terrifying them. They would want to be with me and there was nothing they could do. Besides, no one would have understood a husband's horrifying detachment from such a potentially tragic waiting game.

For the next two years, I lived alone with my fear, a specter of Death in the doorway. As I became accustomed to the routine, and to His presence, I decided to ignore Him. Besides completing the prescribed medical regimen, my treatment of choice for a battered marriage and shaken confidence gradually shifted to a round-the-clock schedule of work, activity, study, and more work.

Bit by bit, over the years which followed, I built a lifestyle bordering on frenzy. To an already frantically busy career, to motherhood, housekeeping and handling the family finances, I added one additional project after another: tending a vegetable garden and fruit trees, landscaping the two acres around our home, then studying and growing culinary herbs, followed by clothing design, and efforts at refinishing and upholstering furniture.

Dozens of picture frames and albums were soon filled with original photographs of my daughter as I tried my hand at photography. Reviving the interests of my youth I took lessons in dressage and show jumping, furiously studied piano, guitar, watercolors and acrylic painting, yoga and gymnastic free floor exercise. I raised purebred Golden Retrievers; enrolled in college classes in linguistics, physics, and chemistry; built a swimming pool and swam laps.

We spent a fortune gutting an ancient four-thousand-square-foot house down to the bare studs and rebuilding from the floor up. Wanting to be part of every phase, I acted as crew boss and managed all the subcontracting. As construction concluded, each room was redecorated and it became a daily race to keep everything from the kitchen to the driveway spotlessly clean.

My daughter, Rachel, was shuttled to every conceivable event, every kind of lesson, museum, outing. She and I shopped to exhaustion so that she should be turned out impeccably. Her teacher commented that, beautifully clothed, with every hair in place, she looked like a model from a children's fashion catalogue.

Celebrations of holidays and special occasions approached the proportions of a Cecil B. DeMille production, with elaborate preparations for everything from Valentine's Day and the Fourth of July to St. Patrick's Day and Easter. At Halloween, no costume was too much trouble: sorcerers, fairies, brides, angels, witches, gypsies, all carried out with attention to detail that would match the standards of the Smithsonian Museum. [Only the year my daughter insisted on dressing as an Adverb did we hit a snag.]

For Christmas we decorated from lamp post to newel post and decked a twenty foot tree with handstrung cranberries, ornaments from around the world and real candles on a scale that would suit Rockefeller Plaza. Underneath ran a replica model of France's "Le Train Bleu," through the artificial snow of a gigantic illuminated Victorian village. I bought and wrapped gifts each year for over 200 people. Thanksgiving, became a marathon seven course dinner. Birthday parties grew increasingly elaborate with gigantic custom cakes and more gifts than anyone could possibly enjoy. The list of deadlines and expectations was endless.

If two projects were good, ten were better. The work day stretched from twelve to sixteen to twenty hours. When Death came looking for me, he would never identify me in the blur. He would never hang on at the frantic pace I kept and would depart in frustration. By the time I was declared "cured," I had established a lifestyle of perpetual activity that could not be easily dismantled.

And, a year after the cure was certain, I collapsed. A kindly, understanding doctor of internal medicine undertook little physical analysis. He just listened. Over the next six months he helped me paste myself back together and warned me to slow down. One would think I'd have learned something from a total collapse. I did not.

When doctors said we could add to our family, I had two babies in two years, both by surgical birth. Three days after the birth of Daniel, I was back at home researching material for a movie about the Apache Indians. Twenty four hours after the birth of Adrienne, I had plugged in a computer in the bedroom at home and sat, in my nightgown, editing a book manuscript. Nothing in the pace changed with two more children. They simply accompanied me everywhere. Life was not just a challenge, but some sort of horrifying, surreal decathlon. I would be the perfect employee, the perfect mother, the perfect wife, the perfect hostess, the perfect friend, the perfect fool.

During this time, my parents retired to Arizona, buying a home a few miles from ours. I know now that they found my lifestyle complex, affluent and unbelievably awful. For the first several years, they said nothing, helping where they could but not wanting to meddle. Finally, my mother couldn't hold it in any more.

"Being with you is like trying to stand up in a hurricane," she said. "You live like a whirlwind, like the Devil was chasing you. You jump up and leave in the middle of a meal, watch fifteen minutes of a movie on television, pace the house like a caged animal. You are continually busy, but not happy. This has got to stop."

But how to stop? I had not only my own expectations to contend with, but also those I had built in other people. People who now thought and even said, "We wouldn't expect this of anybody else, but we know you can do it." This I accepted as flattery, not as evidence of my stupidity and complete insensibility to my physical and emotional limits, not for many years accounting for the price that perpetual motion demands. All these frenetic pursuits had taken on the guise of necessity, not choice. And, like the victim of a highwire electrocution, I could not release my grasp from the source of deadly energy.

Worst of all, the reams of my own creative writing, the pursuit I truly loved, the poetry, the short stories, essays, and book outlines, were tossed into a drawer for "later." If a publisher ever ran out of works to print and came beating down my door, I would be ready. Meanwhile, I would continue to ghost write, to grind out the necessary projects, for others. Nothing arising from my own inspiration warranted concentrated work or thought, was ever refined and offered for print.

Of course, I had good reason for this, in fact, every good excuse known to man, for not turning my full attention to the one thing which would have put a stop to the madness. In fact, the risk of publication, of criticism of the creations closest to my heart, scared me more than death. For, if I failed, I would be still breathing, but defeated.

It took an avalanche to move this defeatist attitude off dead center. After Carreras' performance, I began dreaming again about writing and publishing my own work. The emotion which was jogged loose that night struck a creative core whose existence I had grown to ignore, which had long ago been buried. And, quite literally, I began waking up in the morning with whole poems and compositions complete in my mind, waiting to be committed to paper. Eventually, the preoccupation persisted into waking hours and grew until it absorbed nearly every moment. Finally, I began to build confidence. Maybe each idea would not be my last. Maybe I should get past my fears.

Over two years, I kept my usual job, writing my own material at night. But life began to feel a couple sizes too small, too confining, and then to choke off my air supply. It became painfully obvious I had only so much time to address all the choices I had made that did not fit, did not work, a realization which produced a moderate sense of panic. On the other hand, bits and pieces of ideas jumped out at me from everywhere, adding to my creative momentum. From friends, children, songs, clouds, daydreams. I turned off the television, stopped worrying about the newspaper headlines, and began seeing the extraordinary clues and messages that were left in my path. I began to perceive my own internal workings, to once more appreciate the fiber and muscle of my own unique nature.

At its early stages, I found this process impossible to discuss. People tend to look askance when you throw these kinds of revelations into a conversation about the price of hamburger.

So for a long while I stopped trying to explain and decided to be alone. I realized I was not alone at all when I read a small book "If You Want to Write," penned sixty years ago by Brenda Ueland. She had discovered that young authors who sought her advice often had been taught imitation and phoniness, writing in total ignorance of their own nature and spirit. She explained how they would know the sensation of pushing past these stilted habits to observe honestly, to confront writing with the raw material of their own Soul.

She described the experience in this way,

> You begin to see the world as you had not
> seen it before, to hear people's voices and
> not only what they are saying but what they
> are trying to say and you sense the whole
> truth about them. And you sense existence,
> not piecemeal -- not this object and that --
> but the transcendent whole.

Whether you intend to write books, paint pictures, teach school or drive a bus, this is not a bad way to live. Human beings in every occupation need a sense of themselves, of appreciation for the moment, of respect for the inspiration which is given them. Granted, inspired ideas have some confusing qualities which are sometimes difficult to reconcile. Once they have given themselves, no one and nothing can take them away; yet they still require endless imagination and hard work to sprout from simple seeds to theories, suspension bridges, social movements, electronic gadgets, and even paperback books. Inspiration is demanding, even all-consuming, and does not allow for a leisurely schedule to accomplish this sprouting, does not permit its subject to rest, but teases and torments until it's victim has given it expression and the animus glows from inside the temple which has been constructed in its honor.

An inspired idea cares not at all how difficult it may make your existence as you build a home for its residence. Until the desired edifice is complete, there is no peace. We must all have a healthy amount of respect for that kind of power. For that reason it is impossible for any creative individual to refuse his own constructive impulse. He might momentarily convince himself of an ability to spend a lifetime lackadaisically sorting mail or selling peanuts, but, sooner or later, his own nature will track him down. This makes me wonder about all the young people who are advised by relatives, friends and teachers to "be a lawyer (doctor, accountant, engineer, fill in the blank) because you make a lot of money." There cannot be enough money in the world to compensate for talent that is ignored or, even worse, repressed. For, within the individual, deep in their soul, their spiritual essence rages to be free. Certainly, this must be debilitating to every part of a person -- mental, emotional, physical -- and every life he touches.

It is clear that in teaching children, particularly in formal education, we must match practical goals with the spiritual essence of human beings. This can not be accomplished by a "blanket" sort of education and a curriculum of memorization and the absorption of facts. True education is a process of bringing forth the potential of human beings, of nurturing what was already there, and requires their active participation. That kind of education involves what the late Dan Jordan, Professor of Education at the University of Massachusetts, referred to as "the educational process of becoming one's true self," and relies entirely upon developing the knowing and loving capacities of the human spirit. Jordan focused curriculum on personal freedom which begins with discipline, intellectual initiative, service to one's fellow man, the ability to make value judgments, and aesthetics.

Jordan stressed that information in our times is vast and memorization of any significant portion of it impossible. All of us need, instead, to be able to recognize rhythms and patterns and their validity rather than individual facts, to know how to locate information and evaluate its usefulness. Most importantly, Jordan emphasized the matching of lifetime personal and vocational goals with the true nature of the individual.

The mismatch of education with the individual spirit has preoccupied concerned teachers for decades. Joseph Campbell noted in the television program, "The Power of Myth,"

> Suddenly you hit on something the student really responds to; you can see the eyes open and the complexion change. The life possibility has opened there. All you can say to yourself is, 'I hope this child hangs on to that.' They may or

they may not but, when they do, they have found
life right there in the room with them.

Campbell, until his recent death, admonished students, and
all of us to "follow your bliss" as the surest means of achieving
satisfaction and fulfillment. This has nothing to do with fame or
becoming a millionaire, with owning a large home or expensive
car, or any of the usual definitions of "Success." This has to do
with finding and expressing one's own essence, an ultimate form
of personal happiness, an accomplishment which becomes a
more and more distant goal for many of us since everything in
modern culture encourages people to forget that they have
anything to do with an essence, theirs or that of Nature. We
visualize ourselves as, not just above Nature, but disconnected
and extraneous, oblivious to the golden umbilical cord which
connects us to our beginnings, our being, strength and destiny.

Campbell recommended that each person develop a sacred
place or mental plane in which to investigate one's individual
spirit. This may require a dramatic departure to a remote cave,
or just going to another part of the house where you can shut the
door and be alone, or even some sort of meditation. We have
many options. I came to realize that playing the piano
accomplishes this for me since, even in the midst of chaos, my
mind and spirit fly away on the wings of music, unreachable
until further notice.

With all this new knowledge, I finally determined to make
some contribution to the future of the human spirit. I would
write about an artistic hero, José Carreras, who had so influenced
me. This would be a simple book, something short; perhaps just
a treatise on Art, the nature of the soul and the universe, a
document which would change the course of human history and
once and for all establish the antidote to the tragedy of subverted
genius. This seemed a worthy and manageable cause.

Immediately on the heels of this conviction came a call from
the University of Arizona's music collection curator. Charles
King is a soft spoken and lovely man, a gentleman and a scholar.
He had aided and abetted my overturning of the card catalogue
in search of Carreras material. He had held my hand graciously

and taken the rational point of view as I raved about enobled spirits and the artistic Soul of man.

"There's a book coming out about Carreras," he said in his quiet, archival manner. "Just published."

Ahah! Somebody had thrown together a few facts about the man after all. This might be a starting place for preliminary research. I would cover this basic ground, then contact Carreras with my unique book proposal. And, when I explained my idea about the artist's soul and so forth, he would faint with excitement. The game plan fell into place.

"So, who wrote it?," I asked, picking up pencil and paper to jot the author's name.

"Carreras did."

I sat down.

"Really, what's the title?"

"'Singing from the Soul.'"

Never until that moment had I resented the shared aspect of collective consciousness, the great "OM" of the universe. The soul? The soul? Hell's bells! Carreras wrote my book?!

"Come on, Mama. Be realistic. Whose life is it anyway?" My daughter, Rachel, was trying to get me to see reason through the black fog of my disappointment.

Nonetheless, incredulity blocked anything close to lucid thought. I had been through so much, saddled with this inspirational guest who would not leave. I had finally grown some courage and determined to write, to make something of the moment, and by damn I was writing. What could stop me? Just in time, puffing and out of breath, common sense caught up before I turned the next illogical corner. Wait a second. Hadn't I wanted to know about Carreras? He was trying to tell me. Who was a better authority? This could be the answer. The easy way out. For crying out loud, call a bookstore and buy a copy! The best solution is the simple one.

But first, to cope with the let down, the black pit into which my high flown creative hopes had descended. I determined to regroup with musical accompaniment, with a ceremonial viewing of the Arts and Entertainment network's program which I had recorded, "José Carreras and Friends." The concert, filmed at The Theatre Royal in Drury Lane, documented one of the more hilarious encores of all time. Carreras and his buddies seriously muffed "Brindisi," the drinking song from La Traviata. Bass Ruggero Raimondi had obviously lost a cue sheet from his pocket and, in the course of picking up the phrases for him, Agnes Baltsa, Katia Ricciarelli and Carreras sang "Brindisi" as though they had been in the sauce, to the complete horror of the conductor and total delight of the audience. Wrapped in an afghan with a bowl of popcorn in my lap, I wryly screened the festivities as a memorial gesture. Good-bye Mr. Carreras. I'll buy your autobiography. It's been nice wondering about you. Good luck in your future.

The fun of the encore was infectious and I found myself laughing just as hard as the first time I had seen it. My spirits began to rise again. Something good would come of all this yet. Why, just look at what I had learned so far, about music, about inspiration and creativity, about myself. Certainly, the prolonged efforts of The Uninvited Guest had a purpose.

"That's him?" a voice at my elbow said with skepticism as the last notes of the encore died away and the bowing began.

It was my husband. He had been lifting weights and was pacing through the house in a sweatsuit and sneakers.

"That's him?," he repeated, motioning toward the television. "He's the one you want to write about? The short guy?"

I didn't answer, but took a hard look at the television screen. Short? No, Carreras' remarkable presence towered above everyone and everything. Were we looking at the same picture?

"That's him?" he repeated, "He's got a receding hairline."

This my husband would notice. His own hairline had been receding since college. Alright, to humor him, we would see. I quickly scanned the video backward and, replaying a segment of Carreras singing solo, took another good look.

The halo of an intense radiance around him completely obscured most detail of his appearance. Hairline? What hairline? In fact, against the magnificent glow all I could see distinctly were those deeper, luminous flames: the soft, steady lights in his eyes.

My husband must be ill, intoxicated or going blind. Should I call a doctor for him? He left the room, shaking his head at my stubborn silence. Really, I wasn't trying to be difficult, I thought. But for some reason he seems to be seeing things all wrong. Clearly, something was the matter.

And then it dawned on me. I realized what was at work. He was not changed at all, was just the same as ever. It was I who saw differently now. And what I saw was the truth of a human spirit; a shining wonder visible only to those dead set on enchantment, those happily reveling in the moment, those who momentarily have forgotten themselves and are blithely wearing their underwear on the outside. The Uninvited Guest smiled at me for the first time ever and nodded approval.

Chapter Four

It had been over a year since the Concert at Caraccala. The children teased me, measuring past tense in terms of "B.C.," or "Before Carreras." As in, "Oh really, how many months B.C. was that?" The book, "Singing from the Soul," finally had become available, but only if you knew where to look. Bookstores advised me to contact distributors where I found Carreras' autobiography was being marketed under the descriptive heading, "Farm and Garden Manuals." The distributors advised that I call the publishers and alert them to change the listing of their book. Of course, I got a recorded message, "We will get back to you." And they did.

The lady who returned my call launched into a discourse about the book and its merits, that the color plates alone warranted the price. I needed no selling.

"Yes, I already know I want a copy," I assured her. "Absolutely, please send me one immediately. And, by the way, just in case the orders have been slow, do you know Mr. Carreras' book is registered with the distributors as a farming manual?" She did not and thanked me profusely for the information. Anyway, she said, I would need to send a check and, when the check cleared, my purchase would be forwarded.

The critics, who evidently did not experience all these problems, had received their copies months before and reacted predictably with their terrible, swift sword. The critics, grudgingly it seemed to me, gave Carreras credit for having the courage to discuss his intimate battle with the deadly cancer, leukemia, and for the altruism to create his international leukemia foundation. Never able to leave well enough alone, they proceeded to castigate him for a lack of gossip and juicy kiss-and-tell tidbits from backstage at the opera.

Furthermore, where, they wanted to know, were the scathing evaluations of conductors, stage directors and colleagues? Certainly, Carreras had the inside track on plenty of gore. They had expected theatrical blood to be spilled, innards exposed. Muttered one carping analyst, "Carreras declares tenors 'boring' and then sets out to prove his point."

Of all that exists to discuss and enjoy, why would readers who love opera and the people who perform it look forward to gossip: a toxic and destructive substance ranking right up there with radioactive waste, fluorocarbons and discarded chewing gum? Have these critics ever heard of loyalty, privacy, or even decency?

I sometimes wonder, does anyone besides me find this ilk of art and literary critic creates an extraneous layer of confusion among an otherwise relatively purposeful humanity? Whereas the term "critic" in its original form defined one who indulged in both positive and negative analysis, it now seems to stand for "junk yard dog" as often as not. It's even in the dictionary. "Critic: one given to harsh or captious judgments." Exactly what service do these individuals perform? What becomes of the miles of verbiage they create say, a year, a decade, a century, after the show closes or the book is published? Is it recyclable? Could we make it into gasoline or maybe an organic fertilizer?

Consider the critical contemporaries who found Mozart childish, Chaucer lewd, Blake insane, Monet trivial, Stravinsky cacophonous, Steinbeck common. Yet now we know these men, each and all, by one title --genius-- and recall their artistic themes and lifetime achievements prompted only by a surname.

Who were the critics who sneered? No one remembers. I have a hard time accepting a profession which begins and ends with words, that creates nothing, adds nothing. Criticism, regardless of how witty, does not rank relative to original creative thought and performance. For, without the artist, no critic would exist. I exclude from this discussion, of course, critical analysts of the caliber of Robert Hughes. He is one of those rare individuals who does not equate criticism with cannibalism, who treats his profession as an interpretive process, an art in its own right. And I believe I might trust him with my life in mere recognition of the volume of research this man undertakes before he puts pen to paper.

But, of these others, what motive in these people should we trust? Why do we want their sanction? Wanting them to steer us through the Arts is predicated upon a basic distrust of our own instincts. For the sole importance of the negative critic hinges on our agreement with him to not buy the ticket, book, painting -- sight unseen. His value rests in the supremacy of his opinion, his reaction, over our own firsthand judgment. Why do we defer to this person, respecting the pronouncements of one whose only merit arises from our own abdication?

The public is perfectly capable of exercising its own critical faculties. For example, somewhere around 1975, the Breyer's company introduced an iced cream flavor called Butter Brickle. Your basic vanilla iced cream with pieces of something like butterscotch. This was a best stuff I had ever tasted, yet it stayed on the market less than a year. Not a popular flavor I guess, but I loved it. And similarly, Christian Dior used to make a kind of nail polish called Sharp Brown, a classic tan color. I would have bought it in barrels if it had been packaged that way. When Goldwater's Department Stores sold their business interest at a local shopping mall, nobody would stock it. Not popular enough, too subdued.

You see, after a little while, the majority creates itself and determines what we will and won't have, what works practically and aesthetically. Nobody that I know of insulted Mr. Breyer or Christian Dior with a public notice that Butter Brickle and Sharp Brown had to go and a warning they should never have been so presumptuous as to create them in the first place. These items simply disappeared for lack of interest. Everywhere but in Art we seem to accept the fact that aesthetic tastes differ and the laws of supply and demand will take its course eventually. Based in the premise of "one man: one vote." And if instead a critic had appeared at the store to steer me away from Breyer's or Dior, to clue me in on my lousy taste, I would have missed several small but pleasant experiences.

These examples, of course, do not compare in social consequences with accepting or rejecting the efforts made by artists. For instance, should we wonder that the Arts have a difficult time achieving stability in our society, when we support and fund a cadre of self-appointed executioners with the specific purpose of rendering the creative and performing Arts unmarketable?

Something about the entire concept of markedly negative artistic criticism strikes me as morally disgusting. For, if we accept the premise that artists live to paint, write, sing, to express their love for the world with the vital material of their soul, then what a degraded position the purposely negative critic holds, trailing behind the artist with a running commentary of faultfinding, the judge of someone else's soul. I had thought judgment an occupation reserved for God.

And how is it that this kind of mindless demoralization can go on every day in a world supposedly so advanced and sophisticated? Quite simply, because in the role of the critic, Art meets business. Critics who treat their profession as among the Arts, overcome the temptation to become hatchet men or salesmen. Instead, they fulfill their role as educators of the audience.

But the negative critic, like most of the rest of the business world, does not understand the effect of their superficiality and degraded ethics on the other facets of society and, in fact, considers that people come to Wall Street and Main Street to make a living in endeavors that will never affect the quality of life at home. They are dead wrong. These are not two separate worlds, they are inextricably entangled and the exercise of our ethics and morals at work immediately effects the world in which our children live, and which our grandchildren will inherit.

Somehow our mechanistic, automated way of life has convinced us that we are detached from one another, we are numbers in a computer, we live in a compartmentalized and stratified society in which one neighbor in a global community never meets or shakes hands with the other. And in the media, which often exists completely aloof from the reality of people's lives in a stylized world of its own, the point is wittiness, the lavish turn of a phrase, a glitzy technique that sells newspapers and encourages people to tune in to the evening news.

Tomorrow we will be on to the next headline and yesterday's newspaper will be in the recycling bin.

The premise of this approach is that such a thing as perfection exists and that anyone imperfect constitutes fair game. As adults we know this to be logically ridiculous, and yet our children believe it, and we promote the concept. We leave no room for the variety of the flower garden which constitutes human diversity. For instance, how many young women have died of anorexia and bulimia, from sheer fear of criticism and rejection, trying to look like the glazed, air-brushed and filtered image of a woman on a magazine cover? In all good sense, we know these pictures are phony, yet we allow our children to take them seriously. They never see how these professional productions, or those of movies and television, are staged, audited, edited, into the unreal images that appear before them. Fantasy and reality intertwine into a confused mush we can no longer separate.

With our machinery and technology we can create almost anything, images and objects of mixed substance and purpose, without any ultimate understanding of cause and effect.

I learned today, for example, from a chemist friend that several highly touted brands of artificial coffee creamer contain enough pure sodium to render them highly flammable, explosive. Under those conditions I could presumably whip up a nondairy bomb, a warhead that dissolves in coffee or tea, an explosive that won't clog your arteries. Some of us eat this gunpowder for breakfast because we have been told it's better for us than natural cow's milk. And if that isn't the height of marketing-induced mania, I don't know what is.

Within this creative Pandemonium, among the excesses and nonsequitors of mechanization, we attempt to understand and evaluate the Arts, the raw efforts of real people, who are out of synchronization with most of the rest of our way of life, with the edited, illusionist legerdemain of inventors supported by advertising. And that is why we should guard and protect our artists as a national treasure, as the remnants of an endangered species, who may be the only truly sane individuals left. The only example of how to right our suffering.

For the delusions of mechanization spill over into our everyday lives, poison our intimate connections with other people, since the images we manufacture and project into the television, print on paper, somehow convince us of how satisfied we should or should not be with our personal reality. This falseness and confusion we face literally creates the warlike conditions we often experience in our private lives, as we struggle to overcome a continual conflict between ours and other's imperfections stacked up against a yardstick manufactured on Madison Avenue. As a result, a living and fallible rapport cannot exist among many of us, we allow no such thing as a comfortable or give-and-take relationship. Everything must be by the book, even-up, or no one wants to play.

Mother/daughter, father/son, child/child, husband/wife: we have analyzed, dissected and picked apart every kind of human association until nothing remains which has not been under the microscope. No one has been spared the glare of the spotlight and third degree interrogation. We employ the airbrush technique on everything we undertake, shove our mistakes under the rug, and hope it appears convincing to the neighbors. Crying under the weight of an impossible burden, we watch for signs of anyone else succeeding. Those who rise to celebrity don't last long. We scrutinize their success for cracks, insecurity, human foibles and, on behalf of a petty and insecure public, the media cuts them down to size: our size. We are indeed merciless with each other, with ourselves.

"We gave him a fair chance to respond," say the journalists, "Then we let him have it."

I don't want to live in a world like that. "Fair" is for children's games; "just" applies to lawyers and the judges who make the decisions. Striving to meet those standards is what carries half of America to the courtroom on a regular basis, in search of the ultimate lawsuit, their rightful pound of flesh. No, Fair and Just are not enough. We should aspire to Mercy. This is the quality of interaction which becomes a human being, the finest creation on Earth.

They say that the tallest buildings in a civilization indicate which organism of the society dictates values and standards.

That, in our society, would appear to be buildings like the World Trade Center and Sears Tower, which would mean that commerce rules our lives, that business interests dictate much of the quality of our existence. As such, the interests of business had better change if we expect to live in anything but an atmosphere of strife and contempt. We cannot purchase respect from one another nor value the respect we cultivate deeply enough.

I learned very early how much people delude themselves about the value of money and what it can or can not buy; the incredible bargains a business fanatic is prepared to make. I found out through an acquaintance with a young man who was infatuated with my college roommate and courted her intensely over several years although she never showed the slightest romantic interest in him.

"Forget it," she said, "I am going to be an intellectual, not a housewife."

Regardless, her admirer followed us everywhere and we became friends. It was from his father that I learned just how much some people think money can buy. I only met his father once, at a dinner at their home in Philadelphia. He was a business magnate, a big wheel in the textile industry. We talked about literature, languages, art, life. He asked about my family and academic achievements, inquired what plans I had for the future. A few days later, his son approached me looking shaken and sad.

"I promised my father to offer you a deal," he said. "If I don't, I will never see my inheritance. He said I am an idiot and that he's not leaving his business to me. If you marry me by your twenty-first birthday, he will pay you a million dollars. He will teach you to run the company. Then I will get my inheritance. He is going to call to be sure I gave you this." He handed me a signed promissory note.

I could not believe that anyone would wound their own child this way; not only desperately embarrass him, but also turn his future, his dreams of love and family into a business deal. Did he think he could buy and sell people? Slavery had been dead in America for over a century. It was inconceivable, beyond comprehension. But it was true. And in his greediness and grasping for control, this father could see nothing of his son at all, nothing of a fine young man, a brilliant mathematician, who was hopelessly in love with someone else.

His father never called me because I sent him a letter the next day explaining just who I believed the "idiot" to be. And, in due course, my friend prevailed. He moved to California, invented a new type of computer chip, and became a wealthy man in his own right. He, his wife and children were well and completely happy last I heard. And, in my darker moods, I have hoped that his father's textile plant burned clear to the ground, incinerated without a trace.

As shameful as this incident was, it probably does not constitute the most cold-blooded business proposal of the century. Business has a habit of impersonality, lacking any shred of the sentimental and romantic, bowing always to the practical and shrewd. The race is to the swift; we need a decision - NOW. The business motto of the twentieth century.

Yet the cure for this epidemic seems simple and obvious. Business desperately needs the influence of femininity.

That is the beauty of the Arts. It flies on two wings: the masculine sense of practicality; the feminine ideal of compassion. "The show must go on": and when it does, must be portrayed with care and sensitivity. Instead of commerce and industry absorbing the Arts and teaching brutality, it should be the Arts which leads, teaches and establishes a better standard for the transaction of business.

I believe that lack of femininity in the corporate world is the reason that whenever I found myself at a loss, wondering how people could be so singleminded, ruthless and cruel, I began questioning, "What would my mother do?" Wishing she were there. This is not a plea for Women in the Workplace. God knows I have no interest in adding fuel to that highly charged, perpetual arm wrestling contest between men and women. Men and women differ in their approach to problem solving, to relationships and communication. And it's not a question of competing with the difference, of killing it, but of appreciating and understanding it.

I once heard a revealing story from a psychiatrist who was illustrating the difference in the way men and women communicate. It went something like this:

A husband and wife sit down to read the Sunday newspaper together.

As they settle in on the sofa, the woman announces, "Our iron broke this week. So I'll need to get a new one. I was thinking about what kind to get and that brought back some wonderful memories...."

Without waiting for her to finish, her husband, who has spotted an advertisement in the newspaper for a sale on irons says enthusiastically,

"Look here, there's a sale on irons at this store. Tell me what kind you want. I'll go get one for you."

Now, the wife does not respond to his comment, but continues with her original train of thought:

"Looking at our old iron made me remember how, as a child, I sat for hours with my mother in the kitchen while she ironed clothes. I can still smell that old steaming iron, the starch and clorox she used on my father's shirts."

Meanwhile, her husband holds up the newspaper.

"Look, there are three kinds. One has steam. You want steam? The price looks pretty good."

His wife does not hear him.

"Maybe I should use starch on your shirts. They'd look nicer. What do you think, are they alright the way they are or would you like me to starch your shirts?"

Husband: "I don't care. Do whatever you want. But, the sale's over today. You want an iron? Let's go get one."

Wife: "What?"

Husband: "I thought you said you want an iron. Let's buy this one." Frustrated, he points to the picture.

The wife stops talking and leaves the room. And, realizing that something has gone wrong, her husband follows and, putting his arms around her, suggests, "I know, honey. Let's spend the rest of Sunday morning in bed."

She instantly recoils, "Don't touch me! I always knew you hated my mother and besides, you don't listen to a word I say!"

Everyone present at the time this story was told burst into laughter. This must be a very common scenario indeed among couples. The psychiatrist said the example of this little story comes from many years of figuring out how men and women communicate, what makes them tick. Overall, I liked his ideas because he was not obscuring his explanation with some jargonistic nonsense; suggesting some homogeneous "recipe," or yet another complex psychoanalytical prescription that required anyone to drag their personal issues into some third party's office. He was searching for a simple way for couples to understand, to unify and heal their own relationship.

What we have here, said the psychiatrist, is two people trying to communicate while they have two different conversations. The husband is talking about solving a problem for his wife. He thinks she wants an iron. His wife had wanted a conversation. to tell him about childhood memories of her mother, to check out whether her husband approves of how she takes care of his shirts and of him. He is trying to be helpful, gallant, to show his concern, to be closer in the all the ways he can imagine. She is trying to explain a childhood sentiment, feel reassured and cement a closer understanding with him.

The psychiatrist's point, however simplistic and understated, was that in his vast experience he had noticed four types of communication styles: mental, physical, emotional, and spiritual.

Talking with couples he discovered that men communicate most naturally mentally and physically. Give them a problem to consider and they will go to work immediately on the solution. With a practical solution decided (or failing a practical solution), they will bridge any remaining gaps physically to demonstrate their love and concern. If a woman can't accept their attempts at finding a solution or at offering physical comfort, they're really not sure what to do for them.

In contrast, the psychiatrist's premise stated, women work unflaggingly to put emotional and spiritual bonds in place and keep them there. They generally want to establish emotional commitment and to create deeper spiritual understanding. A prescription does not suit them as an answer. They are looking for a more complex kind of comfort and involvement that tends to have their husbands baffled.

In a way, this may sound like a recipe for a showdown. But, what the therapist was suggesting was that making room for this comprehensive combination of approaches to communication and giving consideration to both should create some very powerful partnerships in the world. It is not a question of right or wrong, intelligence or stupidity. The people in the story are headed for the same destination, but need to negotiate the route. Both want companionship, friendship, affection and a sense of security. It would seem that the key is to treat the differences and discussion less like a civil war skirmish and more like a light-hearted calypso. They need to learn a few basic steps from each other, listen for the music, and try not to step on each other's toes. Vive la difference!

Fortunately, hormones are not an exclusive right; there are masculine and feminine qualities in all of us. And both men and women can learn from each other. But, we tend not to apply our feminine traits in the commercial world, (primarily for fear of being overpowered) and it suffers accordingly, remaining detached and causing trouble everywhere else. My mother comes to mind in visualizing a cure for this situation because she understood the best of both sides and combined them in herself. I grew up knowing her as a woman with the strength and endurance of a stevedore, the knowledge of a professor, the wisdom of a Supreme Court judge, the courage of Daniel in the lion's den, all packaged into a small, feminine person who bore a remarkable resemblance to Susan Hayward.

The fact that my father worked all over the world as an engineer and we lived on a horse farm, placed an incredible responsibility on my mother's shoulders. She could act as midwife to a horse in foal, bring in the hay, drive a tractor, balance the family finances, splint a broken leg, compose a professional oil painting, decorate a home, teach her children to dance, fix a broken pipe, dissect a frog for a science project, correct an English termpaper and a poor violin technique, console a heartbroken neighbor, barter with the butcher, and call it a day's work. Come evening, she could throw on an iridescent taffeta dress, tie up her wavy auburn hair and leave men's hearts panting on the floor at the opening of a Broadway musical.

Periodically, beginning in the year I turned twelve, she worked in politics and traveled around the county, leaving me in charge. I strove mightily to stand up in her shoes, burning dinner, getting trampled by horses, setting the chimney on fire. Trying on her taffeta dress, I didn't seem to fill it out in all the same places. I could have been discouraged by the comparison, bereft of any hope of ever being remotely like her. Yet, she always congratulated and applauded my efforts, made me feel appreciated, encouraged me to keep trying. And that is what the compassion and caring of femininity does for people.

My mother's presence would change the tone of any business enterprise for the better. First of all, everyone would sit up straight, speak distinctly, use correct grammar and get their facts straight. Second, my mother has a radar that detects dishonesty miles away and spots offenders from short range with the eyes in the back of her head. Liars and double-dealers beware!

She would help everyone and teach them whether it was in her job description or not, and soon they would find themselves doing the same. And no one would care who got the credit. Everyone would live up to their potential and she would congratulate them on a regular basis until they learned how to congratulate themselves and each other. There would be no sniveling, but anybody with a real problem would get sympathy, a soft shoulder to cry on and a clean handkerchief. She would know each individual personally, the names of their children, their birthday, the ages of their grandchildren. No one with whom she was even remotely connected would ever want for the necessities of life or lack for opportunity. Everyone would exercise good manners, even if they didn't like one another.

The cruel and unthinking would be made to apologize and only true sincerity would win forgiveness. Hoarders and the greedy would be banished for good. Everyone would be made to think through the long-range repercussions of their decisions on the future of society and the planet. Each person would be required to search their soul and determine whether their own mothers, if they were watching, would be proud of them. All would be expected to wait on themselves and clean up their own mess. Everyone would be greeted in the morning with a serenade and leave at night with an appropriate benediction. And industry would take on an ethic and morality, a sense of stability and comfort, becoming to a Commercial Family of Man.

Until something of this nature occurs, the news stories, the headlines, the nature of criticism, the treatment of children, the understanding of artists and those close to the heart of civilization, will not change much. For the intelligence of people, their strength and inventiveness which generates the material goods of our culture, attempts to dominate the instincts of genius and creativity which are above its understanding. A genius and creativity which are the hallmarks of the essence of Man, which deserve to be cherished and held in our most hallowed regard, which should be an integral part of the way we live.

You will know when femininity has its day. You will pick up the "New York Times," and the front page stories will say:

"We have confirmed a report that all the neighbors in the world have shaken hands and now know each other's first name." "Today all peoples on earth had enough to eat and had the strength to smile and laugh together for the first time in history." "The entire city of Los Angeles has apologized to one another and promised to do better next time."

When you turn on the television the announcer will say,

"Scientists determined today that the Earth is clean and whole again and has been rid of toxins," and "Today families everywhere found enough time to be together." "Meanwhile, researchers have discovered that the cure for disease is happiness and peace of mind."

And our joy will ripple through the Universe until the word comes back,

"This morning, the sun rose upside down and the stars stayed out all day to laugh at the joke."

"Today astronauts approached the edge of the cosmos and shook God's hand. He said, 'Let the people on Earth know I am proud of them. They finally understand. And, by the way, tell Nancy's mother thanks a lot.'"

"Singing from the Soul" arrived by United Parcel Service at 5:30 p.m. on a Tuesday and by breakfast Wednesday I had read everything from cover to cover, from the dedication to the discography. The critics and I agreed that something was missing. We just didn't agree on what it was.

Chapter Five

I was heartened to discover that "Singing from the Soul" did not tell me at all what I had expected to hear. Carreras spoke about many events of his life, his illness, some of his opinions about operatic production, and the vocal method which he described as "singing from the soul." His book was an interesting journal, not an involved discussion of his artistic philosophy and the implications of Art in our world, as I had thought it might be. The future began to brighten. Perhaps an opportunity still existed to interview and write about him, to understand the source of this unusual impact he had had in my life. And, just maybe, to find a way to send The Uninvited Guest back to Carreras, where it belonged.

The Metropolitan Opera in New York City provided an address in Barcelona, Spain, where they suggested I try to contact Carreras' agent. This agent, they felt certain, handled such matters. I wrote a five page book proposal which, without mentioning my strange experiences with The Uninvited Guest, explained the work I hoped to produce about artistic heroism and music. With great trepidation, I placed the document in an oversized envelope, so that it wouldn't get lost in the volume of fan mail, and dropped it into the letter box.

It was done. And the waiting and the nightmares began. Nearly every day I reread what I had written and berated myself. Oh, why did I say that, why didn't I put it another way? This didn't seem quite the right word or punctuation. Why hadn't I taken more time and care to get it right?

Several months went by without an answer. I knew it. I had fouled it up. The letter had been too lengthy and wordy, I decided. I chiseled the proposal to a single page and mailed that. Then agonized some more. Now perhaps I had provided too little explanation, would come across as brusque and heavy-handed.

"This is all wrong," I sighed, "I'm afraid if Carreras ever does read this he'll consider me an idiot. And that will be the end of that."

"You worry too much, Mama," said Rachel. "You're always afraid you don't have enough information or that you haven't explained it right. Your idea of an obscene phone call would be some guy whispering, "Hey, lady, you're stupid." A few more months transpired. I was not going to get an answer. My efforts had failed. And The Uninvited Guest had not let up at all. I was living two lives: the one that was expected of me and the creative one I couldn't explain to anybody, not even myself. The old lifestyle was built around efficiency and rapid response to crises, incisive decision-making power and the creation and preservation of material wealth; the new one I was attempting to create was centered around reflection, contemplation, inspiration and spiritual ideals. As wrong as the old way felt, it had a familiarity and certain compensations including a known routine. Besides, I wasn't sure about trusting my future to the strange emotions generated by The Uninvited Guest. And, it had never occurred to me that straddling this emotional and spiritual fence might be physically impossible.

I was an inspired basket case and suffered another physical collapse. I had felt very tired for a long time. Working all day and writing half the night had taken its toll. The day I nearly passed out with dizziness I told The Uninvited Guest I was giving up. It could stick around, but was wasting its time. I would write no more letters to Carreras or anybody else. There was no hope. I could see I was seriously ill. Our family doctor ordered tests and had results in a matter of hours.

"We need to put you in the hospital," he said. "You have some sort of inspecific virus that is attacking your liver."

I had an immediate negative reaction to the hospital idea; had the sudden sense that if I went there, I would die. Overly dramatic, perhaps, but I argued to go home. Finally, the doctor agreed. My immunities were so low, he said, home might be better, but only if I promised to rest, eat a bland diet, and not do any work. Frankly, I couldn't work. I was too exhausted and nauseated to eat and could barely walk.

For two months, I lay on an overstuffed sofa in front of a roaring blaze in the den fireplace, burning cord after cord of wood, covered with wool blankets and a heating pad, trying to get warm. I felt a chill that seemed to radiate from my bone marrow, bringing with it a horrifying sense of diminishing energy, as though every breath might be the last. It made me afraid to close my eyes for fear I would not wake up again. After a few days I realized why the hospital had scared me so terribly. If I had gone there, I would have had to leave the music at home, and that is where I found the greatest comfort. I played the stereo night and day. The same disc, over and over: José Carreras singing "Catalan Songs." If I could hear it, I somehow felt certain I would be alright. It would be safe to sleep. When I woke up, I would still be here.

My parents called as often as they thought reasonable, suggested second opinions, recommended I consider the hospital again. But as I lay there over so many weeks, completely still, my own captive audience, I began to understand the nature of my internal dilemma. It was not enough to live the life I really wanted on the sly, as though it were a side issue, an occupation for spare moments. It was not possible to keep everything that was welling up inside on the "back burner" for some future moment. I had made token progress, but so many parts of my life still did not work, did not fit, rankled and gnawed and now even threatened my health.

For the fact of the matter, if I could just once admit it, was that at the fundamental base, at a subatomic level, I was nothing but sad and lonely. With hundreds of people around me, in the midst of Fiesta in Rio or at the New Orleans Mardi Gras, it wouldn't matter, I would still feel that way. Because, my electrons were not humming, my quarks not singing and serenading one another. Deep down, everything cried in isolation and despair.

Admitting that kind of unhappiness, that I had so completely missed the boat, felt like failure. So I had put it off.

"Keep smiling and waving," I said to myself, "You have everything there is to possess, you lack for nothing, what do you have a right to cry about?"

But, I didn't have myself. And without me, I would be forever alone, no matter who or what else came along. Inside, my spirit was dying. The light was about to go out; the singing cease entirely. When would I make the decision? When would I take the risk? I had written lots more poems, short stories and paragraphs as they occurred to me and stuffed all of them into a drawer along with the rest, finishing and publishing nothing.

And, if my original idea of writing about Carreras had come to a deadend after such intense effort, so what? Did I have to quit entirely; waste everything I'd done? Had I thought it would be easy? Uninvited Guest or not, I was still locked in daily battle with myself and hadn't gotten much past square one.

Rounding the bend into the third month on the sofa, I was still listening incessantly to "Catalan Songs," when a new thought struck me. I knew what was wrong. I had written to Carreras in the wrong language. How could I be so stupid? He wasn't English, he was Catalan! And, if I wanted to make some complex and heartfelt explanation of this project, it needed to be in a language that meant something to him at the level of the heart. I had a new direction. Hope was not dead. I just needed to get back up, to get busy.

I picked up the telephone from the floor next to the sofa and started making calls. Someone in a city this size must know Catalan. Within minutes, I found this someone at the University of Arizona. Dr. Joan Gilabert (pronounced Joe-ahn Gee-lah-bear), was a native of Barcelona who taught several Romance languages at the college. I explained my project to him and he had immediate interest in it.

Dr. Gilabert was an opera expert. In addition to many other projects he had undertaken, he had translated the libretto for "Carmen" from French to Spanish for the current production of that work at the operatic theater, the Liceo, in Barcelona. I could not have come across a more understanding individual.

"Will you teach me to speak Catalan?," I asked him.

"God, no!," he said, "What for?"

I explained I needed to redraft my letter in Catalan. And if Carreras accepted this idea, I would have to be able to speak the language.

Gilabert laughed out loud. "You don't have to build a house," he said, "in order to find an open door."

If I wanted a letter translated, he explained, he would be happy to help. If Carreras accepted the proposal, we would work out a way to deal with any potential language barriers.

"The letter has to say exactly what I mean," I told him, "It can't mean something else. It has to be precise."

Dr. Gilabert understood and said he would follow my wording as directly as possible. I placed a draft of the letter in his mailbox at the University the next morning and a few days after, mailed a Catalan version of the book proposal to Carreras' agent -- at a different address. That is, Dr. Gilabert had suspected that the address provided by Metropolitan Opera had directed all my prior correspondence to an impossible street number. He called relatives in Barcelona to confirm his suspicions -- and a correct address. Here, all these months, the letters had been headed for a destination that did not exist!

That week, when I returned to the doctor's office for tests, the liver virus was completely gone, without a trace. The doctor said this was virtually impossible, that he had expected a minimal recovery after six months in bed, a more or less complete recovery in a year and that there might even be a chronic residual effect of the virus. But I had recovered completely in ten weeks -- once I had discovered the next logical step in my quest.

This seemed more than a coincidence. I was beginning to get the point of how badly I defeated myself by living a life other than my own, by not turning my full attention to the need to express and create, by not having faith in the inspiration that propelled me. And, what's more, I was growing used to the idea that every step in this process seemed to raise as many questions as it answered. For, now I wondered to myself what had been so critical about keeping music playing as a background to my illness and recovery. Not only had I been desperate to hear continual music, but to hear very specific music.

The risk in praying for change is that you will get it. Certainly nothing makes life more interesting or wreaks more havoc than change. Perhaps the strongest instinct in a human being is avoidance. And for that reason, we must come to the point of abject despair to force ourselves forward past our propensity for routine, no matter how disastrous the routine may be. We must come to the very edge of survival, to the desperation of an animal in a trap before we will pray for change and the frightening array of opportunities which accompany it.

Avoidance is a powerful substance which glues us to habit and to the past. The consequences of avoidance, of refusing to chose what is right for you, can be illness. Based on my experience I would hazard a guess that ninety percent of illness is an emotional or spiritual problem, not a physical one at all. It comes from remaining cut off from the means of expressing yourself or, as Joseph Campbell said, "finding your bliss." And even if you have found your bliss and can't or won't do anything substantial about it, illness will ensue from your refusal or inability to choose wholeness.

Also, some people are toxic to each other and they may as well live next door to the toxic waste dump as insist upon maintaining a close relationship. The best you will find in that type of relationship, unless someone undergoes a radical change of character or heart, is tolerance. Otherwise, these negative ties to other people can consume and paralyze. Certainly, they will do nothing for anybody's inspiration or creativity. If you modify your lifestyle in a way that frees you from a toxic relationship, those who were accustomed to being able to consume and paralyze you will react. They may be irritable, distant, even angry. And, that's fine, because now something that was stagnant and destructive will have to right itself. Meanwhile, you will feel guilty and sad. Why not, you are probably going to have to say good-bye to an old "friend," albeit a toxic one. So get out your hanky and work your way through it emotionally and then move on. You will thank yourself in the long run for following through.

Working out these conclusions made me realize, it doesn't matter if we are offered the world's most astounding opportunity, we will avoid modifications of our routine, even a painful routine. Because, with change, we lose our sense of a center, of familiarity, of a known focus around which our life may spin. And that, to me, explained my affinity for the music, an absolute need on which I could not compromise: I had been on the threshold of giving up everything. Deep inside I knew I was bidding good-bye to a way of life; that what and who I had been were gone. Regardless of how emotionally shabby and detached that lifestyle may have been, I still needed a center, a focal point, to keep from getting dizzy. Something like a ballet dancer headed for a long series of whirling tour jettes. They stay on their feet by establishing a spot at eye level which they fix visually on each revolution. For me, music worked as a similar focal point. As for the specific choice that had to be Carreras because, after all, his was the voice which began all of this.

I have always used music as a way to think through writing projects. This was the first time I had felt I needed it as a means of basic survival. But it worked. And now, I know how to weather even life's major changes musically. That is a wonderful security blanket.

Getting out of a lousy lifestyle into a better one means that sooner or later you will have to face the demons of bitterness and hatred. How did I get myself into this in the first place? Whose fault is this? We demand that the guilty party raise his or her hand. We expect a reasonable apology. Naturally, we can all think of lots of good reasons why someone else is responsible for our problems, difficulties and shortcomings. Any of us could readily pick out a couple people or social ills we would like to blame for our failings. It's human nature. We are very clear on identifying other people's problems. One of the funnier examples of this I had ever heard came from the English Court of Appeal of 1882, when it attempted to draft an address to the Queen in honor of the opening of a new chapel. The proposed draft stated,

> We your Majesty's judges, conscious as we are of our manifold defect..." Sir George Jessel, Master of the Rolls, strongly objected to that phrase and said, 'I am not conscious of manifold defect and, if I were, I should not be fit to sit on the bench." There was much argument and

finally Lord Justice Bowen suggested as a compromise that instead of saying "conscious as we are of our manifold defect," the words should read "conscious as we are of one another's manifold defects."

It is identification of "one another's manifold defects" which makes bitterness and hatred possible, which provides an atmosphere in which they may thrive. This universal sport of blaming others should be banned in all precincts of the world. Bitterness and hatred eat people alive, right no wrongs, and in fact destroy entire communities, even whole countries. Each of us may be relatively helpless in controlling for international problems of bitterness and hatred. Not so in our own homes and communities. There is much we can do. Our individual salvation as spiritual beings demands, not just that we recognize the dense pollution caused by these negative emotions, but that we transcend it entirely.

Transcendence is the attribute of those who live life as an art, regardless of what they do for a living. However, coincidentally, the world-class example of someone who chose transcendence and illumination over negativity and despair we may find in an artist, the magnificent cellist, Pablo Casals. Certainly, here is a man who had every reason on earth to be bitter and to hate. Banished from his homeland in Spain by the brutality of the Franco Regime, Casals was an artist forced to wander the earth, a tragically exiled artistic genius. What a waste!, we may say. Not at all. Casals turned his career into one perpetual benefit concert for world peace. He had perhaps the greatest impact of any artist in our time on behalf of the cause for peace. He used everything at his disposal, speaking out in those countries and cities where he gave concerts, as well as refusing to play any solo programs in international concert halls after 1945 as proof of his personal, continuing outcry, his demand for recognition of the individual rights and freedoms of human beings throughout the world.

How does someone overcome such devastating changes in fortune, such brutality and individualized terrorism? How does one rise above all-encompassing misfortune and personalized acts of hatred?

Casals rose above all of this, paradoxically enough, by means of humility. This fragile and elderly man whom most of the civilized world called "maestro" and "genius" seemed not to have a grandiose bone in his body. "Natural, natural," he chided his students on a recording I was fortunate to have received as a gift, a recording of his candid rehearsal sessions with young musicians of the Marlboro Festival Orchestra. By "natural," I believe he meant not that the students should play with gay abandon, but that the moment belonged to the music, not to the musician. That is how Casals played, as an interpreter, as an ambassador of musical goodwill from another realm, not as a pompous showman.

Just to see him hold the cello was in itself instructive. Even in moments of relaxation and conversation, the cello stayed in his arms, cradled as gently as a dearly loved child. His love was for the instrument, for the music, not for his own glory, or, even in protest, for his own vindication. Casals lived in a dimension which surpassed any poor government's ability to terrorize or oppress him. He understood transcendence. Nothing could demonstrate that more than the statement he made to young students from around the world at his Master Class given in 1968 in Puerto Rico.

Casals spoke of his own artistic hero, the genius who had impressed and inspired even the greatest cellist who has ever lived. Explaining his sentiment about Bach, and in particular about the Sarabande Movement of Bach's 4th Suite for Unaccompanied Cello, he said, "This is the most beautiful thing that has been written in music. Every time that I have played this, and this means hundreds, when I come to this moment I am so afraid and moved that I want to play it on my knees. There are no more notes. This is supreme." And we, each of us, as we discover the artistically supreme moment for ourselves, may also achieve transcendence, and there is literally nothing anyone can do to remove or mar that sense of completeness.

"It is resolved," I told myself, "Somehow, I will have the faith to see this through. I will start making decisions, I will take a stand and say what I think, discard the unnecessary, jettison what doesn't fit and doesn't ring true. I will stop making a career out of things that don't matter, that no one, not even I, care about. I will teach these electrons to sing again."

But, now that I had recovered and was waiting for the answer to the Catalan letter, one additional obstacle arose which must be overcome. I became impatient. I was losing the moment, the proper time to write. I would forget the way I had planned to address the book. No matter how many notes I could get on paper, the ticking of elapsing time taunted me. I was tired of the sense of delay, the feeling of wanting to get on with it. Having no choice but to wait, I began questioning my impatience. Was time really lost or was that my illusion, one of my imagined limitations? I wasted alot of energy, I realized, demanding that life meet my relentless schedule.

Perhaps trusting inspiration also meant that I be willing to let things take whatever time they require. This of course, was not the way of business, the typical reaction of the corporate executive, was not within the guidelines of all I had been trained to do. Executives get answers; and they get them today! But in the case of a creative effort, pressing for answers and immediate response probably wasn't going to help. This project might creep forward over months, years, decades, who knew.

If I were committed to my dream, I would have to creep with it.

Besides, I still had so much to learn to be able to write an artist's portrait. My only ally and teacher was this insistent, unforgiving inspiration and, all these months later, I had yet to unravel the source or purpose of that. I decided to calm down and stop worrying about Time. It would have to worry about itself. I would not allow Time to become a nemesis either. I would have faith that living out this inspiration would take whatever time it was supposed to and that the rest would fall into place.

Time. If we have a magnificent challenge in our Age, it is understanding the nature of time, its effect on our physical world, and our attitudes about how to spend it, how to use it. We have all the phrases to go with our panic: "We're wasting time!"

and "Time is money" we insist. We worry about our Timing. Did we plan correctly, did we Time it properly? In our imaginations, we invent Time Machines and yell to departing Time Travelers: Be sure to have a good Time! It is our obsession. Somehow, we will be in control of this invisible element of the Periodic Table.

We have the simultaneously advantageous and frightening possibility in our century to be able to see with some precision over vast stretches of time, to view history and its consequences. We sense our limitations and virtual insignificance. How will we ever overcome those feelings of smallness and inadequacy? What can we do with this vastness? We struggle for a grasp of the situation.

For instance, who can imagine a Light Year? That, because of the time required for light to travel great distances, what we see from remote ends of the galaxy had already occurred before dinosaurs walked the earth. That what we are able to view through a telescope today with an illusion of immediacy and reality actually occurred eons ago and that those images will be continually followed by glimpses of additional ancient occurrences of which we cannot be informed NOW, as they happen, no matter how hard or with what instruments we look.

For in that world, now is not now, now is many yesterdays ago. And, if we perceive our own Time as well as many varieties of past ones at once, is it possible we can also apprehend future moments in some way? From some vantage point in space, could we logically observe all Times simultaneously? This concept, part of the paradox of the scientific definition of "space-time," has lead scientists to speculate what instruments might be required to tangibly confront and predict such phemonena. Meanwhile, we laymen have learned just enough to realize we know nothing, just enough to make us feel overwhelmed. What can all of this mean about the nature of our world and its purpose?

Working on a philosophic treatise, looking for metaphors to explain the cyclical nature of family dysfunctions, I happened to come across a discussion of the fourth dimension in the science section of "Newsweek" magazine. It was the illustrations of objects projected into space-time, into the fourth dimension, which caught my attention. They appeared to be some sort of eerie time-lapse photography; the strange, twisted and distorted skeletons of angular shapes and spheres propelled through empty space.

"What on earth were these things?," I said to myself.

The answer is that they are not on earth at all. They are illustrations of our natural world attempting to cope with time and space. The article explained in some detail the work of a prominent physicist, Dr. Paul Bancroft, of Brown University. He had actually developed a method of computer simulation which allowed him to hypothetically turn an object through dimensions of time and see the many possible permutations which would be created. The resultant movie, "The Hyperfoliation of a Cube," projected the "realistic" image of the way a cube would appear in the fourth dimension.

I stared and stared, realizing my inability to comprehend a form I had no hands to touch or hold, an object which lingered near, and coaxed me from, the very edge of my imagination. My eyes seemed to cross trying to establish a visual reality, to fix these "phased" objects which existed in multiple times and spaces within a three dimensional concept of time and space. I struggled hopelessly to pin down their coordinates; was constantly adjusting my internal vertical and horizontal hold dials, trying to control for continual mutations of these images. What a completely frustrating exercise. No sooner would I think I had an understanding than it once more eluded me. I was depressed to read on and find there might be as many as thirty two dimensions in Space.

Having read of the concept, I could not put it aside, but continued to mull it over. Finally, I determined to call Brown University and inquire if it were possible to purchase a copy of Dr. Bancroft's film of the cube. A secretary answered at the Physics Department and briefly I explained my purpose in calling and interest in the film.

"Just a moment," she said, "I'll put you through to Dr. Bancroft in his laboratory."

And, before I could stop her, she had rung the telephone through to the lab, where Dr. Bancroft himself answered. I felt like a chimpanzee trying to communicate with Pythagorus, but I muddled through. After all, I had already disturbed and inconvenienced him, I thought, I might as well go ahead and congratulate him on his ingenious research. But, as I have found in the several times I have been privileged to converse with people of great knowledge and genius, he was neither disconcerted nor annoyed. He understood my feeling of confusion and frustration. Dr. Bancroft talked to me for nearly an hour.

He explained how to visualize the fourth dimension and not panic over our finiteness in relation to it. He discussed some of the implications the comprehension of additional dimensions might have for our future. He was so completely at home with these concepts, I began to feel so myself. This was yet another great opportunity for people to edge closer to an understanding of infinity and their destiny within it.

Dr. Bancroft was generous with his knowledge, showing me how to imagine myself outside of our own reality as a means of demonstrating additional dimensions.

"Pretend," he said, "That you are a flat creature; two dimensional, that you live on the wall of the room where you are sitting."

I mentally placed myself in two dimensions on the livingroom wall. He then instructed me to gaze out into the room and see how it would feel for this two dimensional creature to try to cope with the three dimensional objects before it, to try to imagine sitting in a chair; to try to understand the creatures walking, balanced on legs, through the room.

"That is equivalent to the difference," he said, "between living in our world and that of the fourth dimension."

In the fourth dimension, we would have many magnitudes of the capabilities we have here. We would be freed from a bondage, in a sense, of a single length, breadth, depth, and a fixed moment in time. We would exist in limitless time in endless numbers of lengths, widths, and depths.

In Bancroft's film, spheres become elongated ovals, spiraling empty donuts; and the sharp planes and lines of rectangular shapes are pulled and distorted into abstract Picassos, tumbling designs. But, I learned that eventually over great distances and exposure within time, objects finally display repetitive patterns and a comprehensibility that is startling when it appears, that imparts a certain comfort to us creatures, imprisoned within our three dimensional perception. Under normal circumstances, we do not have the benefit of seeing such phenomena played out over great distances, of developing any assurance of their predictability or any feeling of familiarity with them, and that may be why we have developed this habit of pulling everything into our time, our century, our dimensions, of putting everything we can within reach of our five senses.

For instance, as I began to research the history and structure of opera in order to speak more intelligently with Mr. Carreras, I noticed the recurrence of two topics in critical analysis of opera. One was that more and more people are attracted to this art. The other insisted that to keep people attracted, opera must be modernized. The theme of "updating" arose again and again. Update? Up to what date?," I wondered. For, it seems that every day we have a new one. Some operas are already modern, composed in our times. Certainly they do not appear to be the most popular of them. Otherwise, we would not be seeing signs downtown all the time that say, "Back by Popular Demand: 'La Boheme' or 'La Traviata.'" Can this be the only means we have of becoming more at ease with works of art which, in many cases, equate with highly polished antiques: to modernize them?

If I had a lovely Louis XV desk, for example, I believe I would place it in an honored spot in my home. I would sit in a chair in front of it and, running my hands over the burnished finish, would imagine -- Who has sat here before me? What were they thinking and what were their dreams? What sort of person owned or built this piece? I would visualize all sorts of people who had once sat in my place: a banker signing checks, an authoress with her manuscript, a mother with her child, a lover with his letters. And as I shared it with them, the desk would become ever more mine, more known because its history, even an imaginary one, was appreciated. I would not saw off the legs to make it the same height as the rest of my furniture. I would not lacquer it Chinese red to match a picture on the wall. This masterpiece of construction and time would be loved for itself alone.

In this sense of appreciation we of the modern age may overcome our fear of Time. We will never outdistance it; we may embrace it. We may relax and float downstream. After all, we are not really temporal creatures. That is an illusion, the joke of physical existence. We are eternal, in God's image. Our destiny is to return to Him. And, in fact, we have never really left His side.

How fortunate that, in His wisdom, God has given us two magnificent gifts that surpass Time and dimension, with which we may always remember our connection to Him: Art and love. These alone do not alter, do not diminish with the passage of time. Over them time has absolutely no jurisdiction. Their attributes carry them above and beyond the limitations of a fourth, fifth, or twenty fifth dimension. Art and love are eternal and belong to all of us; they are our common heritage from the beginning to the ends of time. Within their precincts, we perceive all dimensions, are complete and united.

I once had the opportunity to participate in an ancient Native American ceremony of the Sundance. Those sworn to this dance followed a drum beat, without food and water for three days. Before dawn on the third day, I was invited to accompany the elder women of the tribe to the source of a stream at a mountain top to bring water back to the dancers. We started out in total darkness, making our way through the misty forest. We would need to return with the water before the sun rose. These ladies, dressed in their pale buckskin fringes, beaded moccasins and feathered hair ties, walked along solemnly and silently; their weathered, dark faces each a living work of art. They might have stepped out of a picture 12,000 years old. These were people from an ancient culture in which everyone sang, danced, painted, hunted, celebrated the changing of the seasons, and tribal and personal ceremonies with every emotion and instinct in them. No one was cut off from their all-encompassing world of the Arts. I admired them that they had managed to preserve a path of joy in life that all their people might follow.

As we climbed, the young man who was guiding us, a cowboy, seemed uncomfortable with the silence. He tried several times to comment on the darkness, the cold. No one but me responded to his chatter.

"Yes, isn't it," I said.

He kept looking toward the Indian women for some word, some indication that he was communicating with them. The strangeness, distance and difference, the gap in understanding, he felt in relation to these people seemed palpable. Finally, in a skeptical tone, he directed a question toward the eldest woman.

"So, when you do this dance, what God do you pray to, what God is it for?," he asked.

She stopped walking and regarded him, astonished, "You mean there's more than One?," she said.

We perceive so many discrepancies in time, culture and beliefs among ourselves that do not exist. What we see is surface: a costume, a hair style, a color, a physical feature. These are nothing that should divide us. We have a place for communication, a place beyond any physical dimension where time bends back on itself, in Art and in love. There we erase all distinctions among us. There, the moment belongs to everyone. It is our birthright in this realm where all of us may dance and sing and celebrate; where all of us may take forever, if necessary, to develop and understand our dreams.

The world of creation and creativity certainly must extend beyond any dimensions that we can see or sense. For, otherwise, where do imagination and inspiration come from? What is the source of our dreams and hope or that overwhelming feeling of love the first moment we see our newborn child's face or feel the touch of someone dear to us? These are beyond poor physical perceptions; the limitations of length, width and breadth or time.

And, if we have it in us to invent anything more, let us all invent a way to envelope ourselves in this ultimate dimension, to live all of us as Artists; to create and laugh in this endless, careless ozone where shapes form and reform themselves, where bills, worries, telephones, weapons, wars and hunger; distort, twist and tear away, unable to keep a hold on us. We will watch them spiral and swirl dizzily as they float helplessly downstream and out of sight, leaving us with our loves and dreams, our endless cautionless celebration. We will live, in the everlasting inspired moment. We will face forever together.

Lately, Time seems to be running backward. Or maybe it's going round and round in spirals. I can't tell. But, for some reason I don't seem to sound my age anymore.

When I answer the telephone, "Hello?," people on the other end ask, "Hello, sweetie, is your Mommy home?"

I look at the phone. "I AM the Mommy!," I say, confusing the issue even more. What is going on here?

I question my own Mother about this puzzling trend, "Do I sound that juvenile, that young and childlike?"

"Yes," she tells me, "And happier and more like yourself than you have in a long, long time.

Chapter Six

"If one advances confidently in the direction of his dreams and endeavors to live the life which he has imagined, he will meet with a success unexpected in common hours. He will past an invisible boundary; new, universal, and more liberal laws will begin to establish themselves around and within him; and he will live with the license of a higher order of beings. In proportion as he simplifies his life, the laws of the universe will appear less complex,...If you have castles in the air, your work need not be lost; that is where they should be. Now put the foundations under them. ...such is the character of that morrow which mere lapse of time can never make to dawn."

Henry David Thoreau

Each June in the southwest desert the sun rises on a morning that brings summer's stifling heat through the front door; a cranky maiden aunt, who will visit for three or four months. Her arrival promises there will be no relief until mid-Fall. Until then, a sweltering climate dominates life as ants scurry along patios in search of rapidly disappearing moisture, rabbits huddle in the diminishing shade of a palo verde tree, and green gecko lizards pant on the garden wall. On such an inauspicious June morning, I decided to transplant the tangelo tree.

A stupid idea, perhaps, to uproot a young tree, one that has made an effort to establish itself, particularly on such an unfavorable day. But this would be my only day off for a long while, my only opportunity for such an immense project, and I had already delayed too long. It was the very fact of the tree's youth and potential that had convinced me to try such a feat as I surveyed the tangelo's position in the garden beside the house and finally admitted to a mistake I'd made a few years ago. A horticulturist friend had advised that I plant a dwarf citrus tree in that spot, but he had assumed I would plant nothing else. By the time I dug a hole for the tangelo tree, I'd already overplanted the area and found just enough space to wedge the sapling in among a multitude of other established foliage.

Nearly a year later, my friend caught my error.

"Oh no," he said, "That's not what I meant. You've already got laurel, hawthorn and gardenia. And those three hibiscus against the wall will become gigantic bushes. A tree just isn't going to have any room, any sun or enough nutrition."

He noted the tree's marked list to the south. "You'll have to stake it up," he warned, "And even then it probably won't grow a supporting surface root structure. It will just drive a single tap root from here to China looking for space and sustenance."

"But, it's just a dwarf tangelo," I told him, thinking of the aggravation of unearthing that root again. "It won't get to much of a size."

"Are you kidding? It will be fifteen to twenty feet tall and yards wide," he said. "Anyway, no tree, dwarf or not, will thrive in such a limited area. It may not even survive. And, best case, you'll have to prune it so far back to contain it, that it will be damaged and never hold flowers or bear fruit."

I resented his dire prophecy and offered him some peaches from a tree across the yard as tangible proof of my gardening talent. We bundled the peaches into a brown bag and he left. His warning gnawed for awhile; after all this poor tree was a living thing and I its keeper. But, in time, the worry about the tree got buried under more pressing concerns. Yet another year later the truth of my friend's prediction stood evident in the garden. The tangelo barely had grown, not even to dwarf proportions, the branch and leaf structure stunted above a struggling root system without the nutrients to support even a single flower.

Apologies do not come easily to my mind, particularly apologies to trees. But throughout hours of digging, remorse was mine. How could anyone be so shortsighted and pigheaded to let a living thing suffer this way? And what about common sense? A few years back, when the seedling had not been so entangled with the hawthorn and mountain laurel, the tangelo could have been transplanted in half the time and with half the effort.

I dug for quite literally an entire day, first to create a place to relocate the tree, then to carefully unearth the single stringy tap root and preserve some sort of protective root ball around it. Lifting the tree onto burlap and into the wheel barrow turned out to be more than my tired arms could manage. Everything crashed to the ground and there lay the thin, white root, completely exposed to the air. What a disaster.

It was nearly dusk by the time the pathetically sad looking miniature citrus had taken up residence in a little orchard on the other side of the house. Particularly in comparison with the robust sweet orange tree next to it, the tangelo's pathology made me cringe. I drove a stout wooden stake into the ground next to the trunk, and as the hose gushed a silver stream of water into the shallow tree well, the leaves appeared to shiver a bit. Perhaps signs of new life, I thought, or maybe the throes of death. Time would tell.

The ring of the radio telephone I'd propped up on the patio wall interrupted my philosophizing. It was my boss. He was calling to tell me that, in a manner of speaking, the windstorm was here and that if I wanted shelter, I had better run for cover fast.

He sounded tense and angry as he said, "I just talked to your husband and he's on his way home to pack his bags and leave."

He was right, of course. I hadn't known when or how this would occur, only that it had just been a question of time.

The details aren't important and, in fact, are no one else's business. I explain any of it, not as a matter of blame, not to find fault or with bitterness. Often such problems have to do, not with ill intent, but with the nature of the species.

Take for example, the Siamese Fighter Fish. I first met one the day that Adrienne, my little one, decided she would like a pet fish. We went to the store and peered into a vast number of tanks, all bubbling and exotic. And then we saw him. There in a bowl, all by itself, swam a gorgeous creature, a red beta, a fighter

71

fish, bright crimson plumes and fins trailing and swirling around him. Neither of us had ever seen anything more lovely. He came with the instructions that he must be in a bowl alone, otherwise, he would feel compelled to fight. We only wanted one fish, so what did it matter?

At home he settled in just fine for awhile. Then one day, the water began to froth, the bowl filled with bubbles. He swam furiously twirling and tossing the blue stones at the bottom. I called the Pet Store and asked if he was dying or taking a fit. They told me he wanted a mate and it was a big decision whether to get one for him or not. The fish expert explained that every couple months, a Siamese Fighter takes on this amorous frame of mind. In the wild, they swim with great grace and show, dive and circle, leap over the surface of the water, fill the sea with bubbles and make a diaphanous, cozy nest of foam. What lady fish could resist him?

"But, be warned," said the expert, "It is different in captivity. Two weeks after you put a mate in the bowl, he will want her out of there. He will drive her into a corner because he needs the bowl for himself, to display all those elaborate fins. It is his nature."

She explained that, in a matter of days, when baby fish were born, the Fighter, sensing the threat of competition growing around him, would destroy their young one by one. You have to feel sorry for such a spectacular fish kept in a bowl. Beautiful and powerful, he is doomed to loneliness because of his innate territorialism. He should be left wild.

The telling of any of this is only important in this respect: to describe an insidious trap and the perilous route out of it. The trap awaits us in our youth, back when we are convinced of the need to fulfill an established laundry list of social obligations, years before any concept of ourselves as individuals is close to formation, when as juveniles we understand neither our nature nor our species.

A relentless march plays as background music to the high school prom, college graduation, a June wedding day, and a first child's christening, all in neat, predictable lock-step order. And suddenly you begin to realize the implications of loving someone

Forever; someone you chose, who chose you, when "everlasting" meant anything past the next fifteen minutes.

For some people it works out. For others, it's like buying shoes that last forever while your feet are still growing. Sooner or later, they pinch. The pinching turns to callouses, then blisters. Going barefoot starts to look very tempting, even essential. For those in pain, there comes a time to decide whether or not to pay eternally for the impulsiveness of youth. In our marriage we had decided enough was enough.

And, under these circumstances, friends choose up sides quickly and irrevocably. My boss had called to cast his ballot. It was obvious that he held me responsible for the outcome.

"You're being stupid. You could have it made," he said.

He reminded me that we had just built a new home, had established solid careers and large salaries, had a garage full of expensive cars, three wonderful children. He told me some day I could retire a wealthy woman and asked how I could consciously choose to lose everything and break up a partnership of fifteen years. The partnership he referenced was not my marriage, but our working relationship. It dawned on me that he was saying that if my husband left, my job went with him.

"I'm sorry but neither of us can tolerate anything mediocre anymore," I told him.

"Why not," he answered, "You've done it this long. What's another month? Another year? Another five years?"

"This is a terrible way for a woman to behave," he warned me, and then added, "Some day you're going to die of your endless need for independence."

At that, I had to laugh. What he now identified as a character flaw was the very reason he had hired me. Nonetheless, in all reality, my husband was a founding father of the company, executive vice-president and a major stockholder. The choice was no surprise. And it did not change my choice. I had recognized the trap, the trap of too much time spent second-guessing my instinct that something was drastically wrong, just because I couldn't put a definition, a name, on what was right. I had waivered, listening to my fear instead of my heart, awaiting too many impossible assurances, requiring an iron-clad guarantee that if I stepped off the cliff into the unknown a large net would be there to catch me.

I paid dearly for my cowardice by living what seemed like someone else's life; observing myself from a safe emotional distance, evaluating my accomplishments dispassionately, mentally updating my resume. Perserverance under these circumstances meant keeping everything in check, in an unemotional reserve, waiting and building strength for the day when the path homeward would be illuminated, when "real life" with its complex involvements, unevenness, risks and passion could begin.

Over time, I found myself longing for something indefinable, something my own. To acknowledge, if only once, what came from my own soul, not from an agenda of crisis and necessity. No more laundry lists, no more one foot in front of the other. Something inside waited to be born. And its birth would bring the answer to the perennial half accusation/half question hurt and angry husbands aim at wives -- "But I gave you everything; what is it you want?" Some things can not be given; they must be discovered.

In my mind's eye, I stepped to the edge of a cliff overlooking the vast, surging blue sea. I felt the wind lifting me. The urge to jump was overwhelming, to dive to the still depths in search of the one perfect pearl, the one truth I sought. This nameless wonder might be on the first coral reef or at the bottom of the Marianas Trench. How would I recognize this indefinable thing? What could it be?

It is that essence which lives behind the light, that spins inside it, at a speed faster than light's 600,000 billion vibrations per second, a reality we have no eyes to see. It is communication at the level of truth, at the level of the soul. It's source is a mystery and we detect its presence when it has already eluded us, trailing a mystic whisper in its wake ... on the way away. The only real evidence we have of its existence is the almost tangible presence of the hope it leaves behind. If I risked all, I might connect with this magical object of my quest instantly -- or never. And, in my search, in my plunge into the sea, I might be buoyed up and carried gently by the waves or swept away, anchorless, a piece of anonymous, homeless debris.

I know now that anyone with an irresistible calling to a creative life steps up to this challenge and accepts it if they are to realize their destiny. That doesn't necessarily mean the end of a marriage -- although it might. But I think it always means resisting the trap of other people's responses and expectations, it means refusing to accept a phony answer, the wrong life, or a prize that is meaningless to you. And most assuredly, it means living with a purpose that transcends your own fear.

Hanging up the telephone, I considered my options for ten or fifteen minutes, then addressed my case in an impassioned monologue to the drooping tangelo tree,

"You tell me from your own point of view. What's better -- to live in endless shade? To die of misery, despair, to be strangled, crushed to death, pruned to a nub, choked senseless, or to stand out here alone and take your chances. In your innate wisdom, what would you pick?"

I heard a step behind me. My husband carried a small bag of a few things he had packed.

"I'll be back for the rest," he announced with certainty, to which my "alright" seemed the only logical reply.

"I'm leaving because I think I'm driving you insane," he said. "Write what you want. Be what you want. Talk to trees if you want."

He acknowledged that when he left, the company management would solidify against me and I would lose my job. He'd make one concession to my loss of a career and the need to support three children.

"I'll stake you for the first year," he said, "but then you're on your own. You'll keep on breathing. You're a survivor."

Then, with a sudden finality, there was one less shadow on the brick garden path in the golden-rose sunset. No, I would not settle for surviving, for barely breathing. Although that might be the barometer of success for some people. Even simple breath comes with its dimensions and distinctions, with telling shades and qualitative nuance. There's the slow, rhythmic peaceful breath of deep sleep. The sigh of relief -- or despair. The shallow, hyperventilated gasps of fear. The elating breath which fills the lungs with not just air, but a love of life. The labored breathing of suffering and struggle. One's last breath on Earth. The slight staccato of a body filled with passion. The breath held in terror. All alive, to be sure, in a relative sense. But with varied purpose and radically different quality. No, survival was not what I had in mind. I'd choose from the whole gamut of possibilities, survival was nowhere near enough.

From a chair at the edge of the garden, I saw my husband's car disappear down the road. Maybe in a while I'd start crying. In this bone-dry heat I'd probably dehydrate from the loss of moisture and, noticing the buzzards circling, the neighbors would investigate and bury me under the lemon tree.

But, as I often find in the garden, particularly under the influence of a spectacular southwest sunset, all dismal thoughts soon evaporated. I rose to find some B-1 vitamin concentrate for the tangelo. B-1 does wonders in preventing transplant shock. The little tree looked pleased although its leaves still drooped and curled at the edge. I unearthed a bottle of multi-vitamins from the medicine chest for myself and swallowed a few with a cup of tea. Some transplant shock formula seemed in order for everyone.

As darkness descended, I took a last look at the shriveled, struggling tangelo and imagined its once-cramped tap root screaming with terror at the thought of uncurling itself in the large hole I had dug to accommodate future growth.

"I know how you feel. Be strong," I begged, "Don't let me down." And, amazingly, the little tree didn't.

In the Fall, my horticulturist friend visited again and, as always, received a tour of the garden. We stopped at the tangelo. Over the summer, it had doubled in size.

"A new tree!," he said.

"No, transplanted." I explained. "Remember the tangelo seedling, the one too cramped to grow? I moved it in June."

"June, good God, it should have died," he said in pretend horror. "What possessed you to do that?"

"It was time," I said, "Time to move or die trying. I'd say it was worth the risk."

"Apparently your instincts were right," he assured me, "You should see flowers and fruit by Spring."

His words were once more prophetic. And among the trees of fruit and flowers, I ran barefoot down the homeward path to the Sea.

Chapter Seven

I invented solitude, sun in my face and iced tea on the
    lawn,
Life's simplest pleasures spun in shining threads to form
    a golden skein.
I discovered loneliness, vibrating silence and days that
    never end;
Hours hanging tasteless, draping shadowed corners that
    shade a funeral pall.
I have traveled solo, a heart beating under mine, waiting
    to be born,
Quietest of breathing, a world strung between the other
    world and this.
And I have known the Oneness of leaning down inside
    to kiss the cheek of God,
Peace overflowing in the oceans of the soul, the rivers of
    the mind.

"Solo"
by Nancy Warren

All down the path to the Sea I prayed out loud, "Oh, God,
don't let this be a stupid decision. Don't let me hit the rocks.
Don't let me forget how to swim. Don't let me wash up on some
cannibal island. Don't let me lose my nerve. God, I'm only one
and I know you have so many to look out for. But, please give
me a clue... What is this all about?" And then I was in midair.

On my fall toward the Sea I had plenty of time for reflection.
Even my family didn't know where I was, what I was doing. I
had rarely left them out of anything, always asked their opinion.
And now, when I drowned and washed up on a foreign shore,
they wouldn't know where to begin to look for me. We had
always stood so close together, making it impossible for the
world and its problems to squeeze between us. We had always
stuck up for each other, protected each other.

It was a family ethic I had learned early in life; one that was important to all of us. I had learned it from my brother, Bud, who was born two years before me. We liked each other from the start. He took me everywhere with him and I was his adoring slave. He had qualities unique for a child, intelligence and gentleness; a wonderful combination of traits in anyone. And everything he learned he tried to teach to me. He was born with a brilliant photographic memory that instantaneously memorizes and catalogues all that he reads, hears or sees. He can quote nearly verbatim from books and decade-old conversations. Even today, if I want the answer to a question, I'll call him. And if he has ever read about or heard about the subject, I may have to wait a minute while he flips through his mental encyclopedia, but he will have the answer.

As a child, I never imagined that not everyone had the same appreciation for my brother's brilliance. I knew nothing of his troubles in life until I started first grade, an occasion for which I was dressed to the gills in organdy and pink ribbons and patent leather shoes. I cried if I had to wear overalls and drove my mother crazy with starching and ironing. And each day, I skipped off to school looking exotic, holding my big brother's hand.

On the playground came my first revelation of the sort of treatment my brother could expect as the class genius. He was in the third grade and boys a year or two older liked to tease and bully him. I was astonished and enraged. I watched this procedure for several days, burning inside. He was so kind-hearted, he had no idea how to respond to bullies. It would never occur to him to retaliate or hurt anyone. Finally, when he had been pushed up against the school wall by one particularly obnoxious kid, I walked up to the offender and addressed his back, "Excuse me."

He turned, "Yeah, kid, what do you want?." And, organdy flounces and all, I punched him flat dead in the nose.

Within seconds, blood flowed everywhere in a scene of carnage not soon to be forgotten by the fourth grade boys of Horsham Elementary School.

I would have done anything for my brother, my ultimate hero. He graciously included me in all his science experiments. At his instruction, I dragged home the local roadkill, half-squashed pheasants and raccoons, for his taxidermy projects. Under his command, I stabbed myself in the leg and donated blood for microscopic analysis. He was Kepler, Galileo, Archimedes, Einstein, everything I wanted to be.

All of it must have looked comical to those unfamiliar with the religion of brother-worship. For instance, on the day I got sent to the principal's office by my first grade teacher for kissing a boy. The principal was sympathetic but strict,

"Don't kiss boys," he said. "They have germs."

This was news to me. But germs were something I knew all about.

"Don't worry," I told him. "Most germs are benevolent. My brother said so."

He looked flabbergasted.

"He saw them under a microscope at the Franklin Institute," I explained. "Really, they're alright. My brother said so."

Nonplused, the principal sat there speechless, so I went on.

"We all need germs. You couldn't be alive without germs. My..."

"Yes, I know," he said, "Your brother said so."

He sent me back to class.

All through school I heard the same phrase from teachers, guidance counselors and sports coaches.

"You must be Buddy Warren's sister," they all said. "We will expect great things of you."

I gave it my best shot, to such an extent that my mother joked, "Let's hope Bud doesn't go out for football, we'll have to buy Nancy spikes and shoulder pads."

The year Bud started high school and joined A'capella Choir I watched him live my dream. He had become one of a group of students with very high musical aspirations. And my brother had a beautiful, mellow baritone voice which impressed the director. Vocal ability alone was not enough, however, membership required citizenship, academic excellence, social skill. Even so, he qualified without the usual rigorous auditioning. He was invited.

The A'Cappella Choir connoted the pinnacle of success at the high school. They studied music as a major, with two daily practices, morning and afternoon, preparing for a year round concert series that took them all over the region. They were celebrated by the community, included in many professional music events in the Philadelphia area, and regularly honored and awarded for their performances. Authoress, Pearl Buck, a parent of several students and a local celebrity, feted the singers at an event in her home.

Auditions were held in a series of eliminations with public announcements of those excluded, those chosen. As horrifying as it all sounded, I decided to try out, preparing by listening to my brother and practicing with him throughout my years in middle school. It was three years from the time I began practicing that I completed the audition process and was, lo and behold!, accepted. I not only qualified but would sing in a quartet for a series of church concerts at Christmas. All summer long I walked on clouds, working out my parts in the sheet music, waiting for school to start. But when it did, I enjoyed my glory for only four months.

Each year, the choir presented an operetta or Broadway musical, to raise money and promote its many talented vocalists. Music directors from several prominent universities were said to scout the performances for scholarship prospects. For three years, my brother had understudied the lead roles -- missing out on other parts -- with the promise that in his senior year he would sing the lead. Through "Oklahoma," "Mikado," "The Music Man," I was his faithful piano accompanist and learned them all right along with him. A confirmed alto, I croaked my way through the soprano duets with him until I was hoarse. For "Music Man," my mother, sister and I filled in all the extra voices for the barber shop quartet, an octave above the score.

When the year's musical was announced, my brother was devastated. Everyone knew it was to have been "Guys and Dolls," with him singing the long-promised lead. I already had Sky Masterson's role memorized. But instead, "Most Happy

Fella'," was the choice, to be cast as a showcase for a tenor. Then we discovered the director had convinced a private student of his, a tenor, to move into the school district for the year, promising him that season's primary vocal role. I went berserk. I decided to protest and stormed into the choir director's private office.

"You lied to my brother," I told the director. "I quit."

He was astounded, disbelieving. No one had ever quit his prestigious club.

Without looking up from his desk, he said in a quiet superior tone, "You can't quit once you join."

"Alright," I said, "Then I just won't sing."

He ordered me back to the classroom. The matter went before the school principal, then the school board, and became known as the Warren Incident. Meanwhile, I lived up to my promise and did not sing a note. Eventually, it was decided no one could stop me from quitting if I wanted to. I had won. And lost my dream.

A few weeks later, when I had moved my things out of the choir room to a regular hallway locker, I discovered a letter taped to my locker door. It was from the school's orchestra conductor, requesting that I come talk with him. I found him in the rehearsal hall.

"I listened to you practice with the quartet at Christmas," he said. "You have a good ear. Almost perfect pitch I think." He picked up a large instrument case.

"That helps with an instrument like this," he said, and opening the case, handed me a French horn.

When children pick instruments to play in the orchestra, he explained, they all want to play the melody. French horn was generally a harmony part.

"As an alto," he said, "You already know the melody isn't everything."

I was, of course, aware that without the contrasting tones behind it the melody has no life. He told me that the French horn as a solo instrument could be incomparably beautiful.

"This is the instrument for you," he said. "Try it and I'll give you private lessons until you can join the orchestra."

For three months he taught me privately after school. He was right, the French horn had a lovely sound, and I soon joined the orchestra's daily practices. Four months after I started he invited me to participate in a regional honor band audition. "Just for fun, because the experience is good for you." Both of us were shocked when I won a chair.

"Look at this, eighth chair of eight," I pretended to complain to him.

"When you've been playing such a short time, be glad they don't tell you to sit out in the hallway on the floor," he said.

He never mentioned the incident with the choir until nearly a year later. Then he told me it was important for people to stick up for their principles, even if it meant giving something up. He had respect for that, he said, and promised eventually it would all rebound in my favor.

The future holds many answers, and seeing the situation play over time, I realized that once more, he was right. Learning to play French horn taught me to transpose music which later landed a job working for the music department during my university years. There I met music professor, Dr. James Zwally, whose wonderful stories about his own college escapades with classmate Leonard Bernstein served as the inspiration for a piece I wrote for the college newspaper. The article got great response and the newspaper funded me to write an entertainment column. As a result, while still in school, I was able to interview and write about Smokey Robinson and the Miracles, The Supremes, Charlie Callas, The Righteous Brothers, Rich Little, Dione Warwick and a multitude of other popular performers. My senior year, an international resort hotel chain hired me, based upon my columnist experience, to write public relations pieces about upcoming attractions in their night clubs and an in-house entertainment newspaper. If I'd sung alto instead of learning to play a horn, I'd have missed all of this.

In retrospect, my experiences with risking it all and starting over had not been so disastrous. And, as I sailed off the cliff toward the waves, remembering that didn't hurt my spirits a bit. Still, I was older with much larger responsibilities and a great deal more to lose. And I recognized more than ever before the need for moral support from my family.

Although well past the point of no return as I plummeted toward the Sea, I decided to talk with my father, explain my dilemma about this book business and the practical and creative risks in the offing. He would give good advice. He would respect my dreams no matter how improbable. We have a comfortable relationship, an unusual and distinctive rapport.

In fact, I believe I was born expecting to find Daddy here. We laugh the same laugh; cry the same tears. We are connected below wherever roots go. When my brother, sister and I were growing up, my father traveled constantly as an electrical engineer, an industrial construction expert. Switzerland, France, Italy, Venezuela, Brazil, Curacao. Sometimes for a year or more at a time. Telephone calls were expensive, connections delayed and of awful quality. All we could do was miss him. And yet, I never felt distant. If I closed my eyes, I could sense him there in my most vivid childhood memory. In my mind, I would always be eight years old and holding my father's hand in a sea of waving grass as the neighbor's pinto horses galloped, bucked and tossed their manes, cresting the hill into the next field and disappearing out of sight.

For at home he was a gentleman farmer. We both still miss the farm and plant things in every suburban patch of dirt we can find, and in pots everywhere. We both love books, dogs, horses, garlic, chocolate, good jokes, good coffee. Both have a side that will always see the world like a child sees a new bicycle.

Daddy has teased me from time to time that I am the only person he knows who travels with him in a car for three hours in complete silence. Neither of us speaks a single word. At our destination, we say good-bye and go our separate ways. We have never felt a need to entertain one another; we just don't need many words. We are together. We know. We are friends.

Yet, if I wanted to, I could tell him anything and even if he didn't answer, I'd know he understood. For somehow without all the verbiage and discussion we are connected; we look out for one another.

Two years ago when my father underwent treatment for a bacterial blood infection things looked very "touch and go" for a while. Leaving him alone at the hospital took every bit of faith I had. But Mother and I had spent too many nights sleeping in arm chairs next to his bed, jumping at every noise. To convince her to go home to a decent bed, I had to follow my own recommendation. The first night we resolved to sleep at home, I awoke at two thirty in the morning with a horrible feeling of panic. Something felt terribly wrong. After ten minutes of worrying and pacing I called the nurse's station at the hospital.

"I'm worried about my father," I said. "Can I come down there and stay tonight?"

"He's fine," she promised. "I just checked on him."

I begged her to look again. She insisted it was unnecessary, but finally agreed in order to calm my nerves. It was minutes until she returned. He had pulled an intravenous line apart in his restless sleep and blood was spouting from a vein all over the bed.

She was stunned. "How did you know?," she asked.

I'm not really sure. But later that week we repeated the performance. The nurses had discussed my premonition among themselves. And when I called again, questioning his well-being, the nurse on duty went immediately without argument. Daddy was allergic to the pain medication they had given him and, in delirium, had struggled out of bed into the hallway dragging the intravenous equipment and bed clothes with him.

In the past few years, when my life began to shred into pieces, I think my father suffered worse that I did. There was no nurse he could call to fix it for me. The day I determined to talk to him about my internal struggles, my future, I had said only the first few words when he threw his arms around me, hugged me and cried. It seemed so unfair, he said. And he felt so completely helpless.

For, suddenly, my marriage and career were gone, and many long-standing friendships at work along with them. Only a few brave souls were not afraid to lose their jobs too if they remained friends with me, and this in the worst economy and employment market the country had seen in years. Our newly-constructed home was up for sale as part of the divorce settlement. I had no firm plans for the future. It certainly seemed my usually orderly and efficient existence was a total mess, even to the most casual observer.

Worst of all, my loyal companion of fifteen years, my golden retriever, Montana, had developed throat cancer and had to be put to sleep. I had just buried him that morning at the foot of Kitt Peak, below the astronomy observatory. I thought he would enjoy a haven for stargazers and dreamers, as we had been.

Witnessing my father's emotional reaction to discussing my problems I didn't have the heart to tell him about jumping into the Sea, my dilemma about Writing, Artistic Heroes, Carreras, Music and The Book. That I woke up scribbling poetry and paragraphs everywhere as they tumbled from my dreams. He might think that on top of everything else I had gone mentally around the bend as well. Yet, in all the chaos, this new inspiration was what consistently demanded front and center in my mind. In a way, it was my life raft, my hope.

I thanked Daddy for the hug. It was what I needed most. And I told him I was beginning to feel there must be a reason that everything I knew and had counted upon had been blown away in a vicious emotional windstorm. He advised that we would have to wait and watch and try to see what came next. I agreed, but neither of us could ever have anticipated what that next momentous event might be.

I think I know now why they say "It's always darkest just before the dawn." This had always sounded like an illogical, or at least mythological, observation. If the sun was officially on the way, in what practical or philosophic way could it be darkest? In retrospect, I realize the truth of the saying, for despair had just given birth to abject hopelessness when the sun miraculously appeared, as if out of nowhere. And, as the fable predicts, just before the luminous dawn there was to be one final, darkest moment, one more seemingly unbearable loss.

As the last remnants of my security blew away in the windstorm, my father's best friend, my favorite uncle, died of heart failure. My Uncle Ted was the most completely kind human being I have ever known. At his funeral you would have thought he was at least the president of the country or a major celebrity. Crowds of people turned out to pay tribute to him. And everyone said the same thing. He had nothing but good to his credit. He was generous and loving to a fault. He never had a bad word for or about anyone. He was loyal, gentle, hard working, totally honest and trusted by everybody.

Uncle Ted and I had formed a mutual admiration society early on. I adored him from infancy and, over the years, he had a standing joke with my father that he would trade two of his handsome sons for me whenever my mother could get my suitcase packed. In particular we shared one great love: music. When I started studying the piano at the age of seven, he was my most enthusiastic supporter. He wanted desperately to play and had tried various courses as an adult with no success. So he cheered for me.

Coming in the front door, his first words to me were always the same, "Play something for me." And, as I matured and my repertoire expanded, he would listen by the hour. I was no Franz Liszt, but I may as well have been as far as he was concerned. I was nothing if not enthusiastic and played our mutual favorites -- Chopin and Rachmaninoff -- like I'd never heard of "pianissimo" or a metronome. My mother would threaten to hang up one of those Old West bar room signs: "Please Don't Shoot the Piano Player, She's Playing As Fast As She Can."

Even so, when I would turn to ask his opinion I'd often find him cleaning his glasses, wiping tears. The technique may have been that bad, certainly it was not that good. Still, my playing must have meant a great deal to him. When I was grown, he could never understand why I didn't drop everything and study music. He would have, he said. But it didn't seem practical, logical, sensible, to me. And he didn't press the issue.

He visited us last the summer before he died. He and Aunt Margie and my parents had been on a trip to the Grand Tetons. Uncle Ted and mother sang, they said, for the entire length of the Rocky Mountains. And when they got home I had anticipated his first words, "Play something for me," by working on an arrangement of Rachmaninoff's "Eighteenth Variation from Rhapsody on a Theme of Paganini," just for him.

When I had finished it and he had applauded he asked, "You're working at an office with computers?" I nodded.

"Do you like it?," he wanted to know. I shrugged. Not really.

"I still say, your heart belongs to music," he said. "If I were you, I'd go where the music is."

Then he snapped a picture of me at the grand piano. It was the last time I would see him. It wasn't that I didn't take his advice seriously. What music? Where? Certainly, I was no concert pianist. I played for fun, for my children, for him.

The day Uncle Ted passed away, my father was more distraught than I could ever have imagined. He could barely speak without strangling in sobs. I know he had counted on my Uncle as the representation of goodness in the world. And now, in the midst of all my personal turmoil, worries that already had my father completely beside himself, Uncle Ted was gone, seeming to take all light and hope with him.

Two days after Uncle Ted's death, I received a phone call from my mother. She wanted to know if I could come down to the house.

I went. As I walked in, the difference in atmosphere was tangible. The weight had lifted, the clouds disappeared, the sun shone. What had changed? Neither of my parents spoke right away. They seemed to be weighing their words. Finally my mother began.

"Your Uncle Ted came to see your father last night. He wanted to talk about you."

It took a moment for the sense of what she told me to sink in. I'd have said they had to be kidding, but the looks they gave me were no joke.

"Why?," was all I could ask.

My father told the whole story. I could see his strength and confidence had returned. He shone with an aura of peace and calm. He said he had been sitting in his bedroom the night before when he realized Uncle Ted had entered the room and stood before him. His purpose was to tell my father to stop worrying about me and to leave a message for me. It wasn't so much the words as a sense, a feeling, my father said. And, he could most nearly explain the message in this way:

"Everything is as it should be. Your life is upside down for a reason and will turn out for the best, better than you could ever imagine. You are headed in the right direction. Your dream is there and you will find it. Don't underestimate yourself, and don't be afraid."

And finally, he said, "Tell her I have always loved her and I always will."

"He is your guardian angel," my father said, "He told me he will always be there to protect you."

When I plunged off the cliff over the waves, I had prayed with all that was in me. I had hoped for a breeze to carry me away from the rocks, calm waters, sunny skies, courage; but I had never dared hope for one minute to be borne up by an angel. And now, miraculously, on the strength of my Guardian's wings, we skimmed the surface of the Sea together, silent, without making a ripple.

Chapter Eight

I descend a little below the earth,
To enter a church whose threshold lies beneath
History's rubble. History, I say,
Is only two feet deep, but we cannot shovel it away.
From the smoking altar a woman wheels slow
As a star, questioning in a tongue I do not know.
I answer in the tongue I do not know.
Then she turns to the mosaic virgin
Dozing on the wall like a map of Asia. "Virgin,"
She sings, "You who are famous for charity,
Do not from this stranger withhold charity."
She reminds the lady how She brought
A lily invisible into a Rose Incarnate.
"This man's wife," she sings, "has borne him no child.
Send her a child." I want to say, "No,
Lady, let us all die, let there be no
More of life. We are all too tired." But I say nothing,
For the Virgin now is smiling like the first Asia, as if nothing
Had ever happened. And the woman, singing no more,
Whispers, "Pray now and remember to ask for more
Than you deserve. The virgin always favors outrageous
Requests."

Behind her the door opens to an outrageous
Film of sky where a uniform flattens like a photograph. Ashamed,
The officer explains he has come for this woman who has shamed
The mayor and put off the tourists. She is, he sighs, quite mad.

Alone, I remember to pray for too much: "Let me also, Virgin,
let me also go mad."

"The Prayer"
Radcliffe Squires

Much of the world considers angels rare, esoteric and invisible except, perhaps, for the monastic residents of Mount Athos, a steep and forbidding peak jutting above the cliffs of a twenty-five mile long peninsula projecting from the coast of Greece. The tiny hermitages dotting the crags of Athos and the central monastery itself have not changed substantially in over a thousand years. To visit the mountain is to step back into the Middle Ages, back to a moment in time when William the Conqueror's exclusion of women from monastic premises was taken seriously, when monks lived silently and ascetically, back to a time when Angels trod where they pleased and when angelic intercession was not only welcomed, but expected.

Here, in recent years, a visiting tourist, came upon a blind and nearly deaf monk feeding crumbs to birds and, not wanting to frighten the old man, announced, "Eimai Anglos," (I am English).

The elderly monk was pleased and unsurprised, "Enais angelos?," (An angel?), he smiled and raised a hand in greeting. Why yes, of course.

Athos may be the one spot on earth that remembers and understands angels. Which is probably why I knew so little about them and had no inkling, really, what to expect from an alliance with a guardian angel. Was he here now in the room? Would he speak to me? Would I see him some day? I seriously thought that if an angel, even a familiar one, appeared to me, I would first faint, then die. My father confirmed that his own experience had been terrifying, although he ultimately was left with a very peaceful and intensely wonderful feeling.

"I am happy that your uncle sent such a comforting message and that I was the one to deliver it," my father said. "But, if it doesn't happen again, that's fine with me."

Mostly, I worried if my angel were missing out on other more important duties by spending his time protecting me. I had to know what to think, what to believe, about all of this. How fortuitous that a woman named Sophy Burnham had already done the research and written "A Book of Angels." I soon found out my father was in good company. Angels have appeared regularly throughout history to the saintly, the artistically and philosophically inspired, and to the pure in heart (not surprisingly, children).

Every religion throughout the history of man speaks of angels in the same way; as God's protection, as His messengers. Many angel stories Sophy Burnham collected from contributors to her work sounded nearly identical in nature to the experience my father described; that his visitor appeared suddenly, as if in an intuitive flash through a telepathic communication, in an encounter in which he was not even sure that they actually exchanged words, but in which he understood and remembered everything with absolute clarity.

His experience was echoed by famous men such as Dante, Milton, Goethe, the poet William Blake and George Washington. In fact, an angel had come to Washington at Valley Forge just to comfort him and assure him that his revolutionary army would prevail.

St. Thomas Aquinas spoke with angels, he said, and wrote what he was told of their existence. Aquinas perceived them to be some form of pure intellect and overpowering inspiration. Angels have nothing in common with ghosts, he said, confused spirits unable to release themselves from old ties to a former earthly existence. Aquinas characterized the birth of an angel as the moment when a specially-chosen Soul, either at death or at inception, is privileged to view the face of God, and never again looks away. An angel sees ever after, said Aquinas, through the eyes of God, in an all-encompassing and instantaneously comprehending way.

They represent the ultimate form of inspiration to human beings; the inspiration of a divine presence delivering a message from God. Of everyone I have ever known, my Uncle Ted would most appropriately fulfill such a responsibility. He is certainly one who should be privileged to see God's face.

Best of all, Aquinas explained that angels exist in all their capabilities and within all times and dimensions at once, in a complexity of activity that we can barely imagine. I felt reassured that with such a range of motion, my Uncle would accomplish all that he needed to and would not have his attention entirely focused on me. And I was well aware of my mother's relief, in particular, that I would finally have someone to look out for me on a permanent basis.

I seemed always to be at the brink of disaster for one reason or another since I had moved away from home years back. For instance, the day I got a driver's license by mistake. I hadn't wanted one because my mind always seemed to be wandering and I was afraid of running someone over. But, eventually, I had to drive to get to work. I intended to try the driver's test as a dry run, a preview, expecting to fail, nervous to the point of tears. The written test score was a catastrophe; the behind-the-wheel test even worse. For some God-awful reason, they gave me a license anyway. I was terrified and refused to drive home, but the friend who had escorted me to the test site, insisted I'd be fine and left. Somehow, I navigated the highway stretch but, once back in the city, immediately took a wrong turn down a one-way street.

Careening away from oncoming traffic, I drove as far as I could in the parking spaces, then quickly hooked a right turn into a deadend. A patrolman who had watched all of this with his heart in his mouth, pulled up next to me and asked what in the world I thought I was doing. I explained I had gotten a license that day but was positive I didn't know how to drive. He leaned on the hood of my car and laughed hysterically; then took me home. I expected him to want the license back. Far from it. Instead, he taught me to drive. And, every morning that week, he followed me to work until I figured out how to get in and out of the city without killing anybody.

Even more hair-raising, I had lived in an apartment on my own for just a few months when a man picked the locks and broke in while I was sleeping . Something about his presence in the room woke me and, seeing his shadow on the wall, I flipped on the lights and confronted him. In facing this stranger, anger overcame any fear I had. Mindless of the fact that I wore only a brief nightgown, I furiously ordered him to sit in a chair and, in this preposterous costume, proceeded to lecture him about his obnoxious behavior and terrible manners. Then, I opened the door and told him to leave.

He never said a word except, "Sorry, lady," in some unrecognizable foreign accent. Then he left. I ceremoniously refastened all the locks he had just picked and went back to bed.

The next morning, the police came to my door. Why hadn't I called them, they demanded to know? I explained the intruder had looked sorry enough. He said he was sorry. They explained he had set fire to an apartment building under construction across the street and held up a drug store at gun point after I threw him out. Had I known he was armed, they asked? I hadn't. Did I realize he was insane, they inquired? I didn't. As it turned out, he spoke only Greek and never understood a single word I had said to him. The only explanation they had for his not shooting me was he probably thought I was crazier than he was.

Later on, there was the time I camped out overnight in "that cute little cave" on the Appalachian Trail that turned out to be a rattlesnake nest; or the day I washed out to sea in a storm on a one-man sailboat and was returned home by the Coast Guard with the distinction that "she's the only person we ever saw sail a boat upside-down, standing on the keel." Or maybe I should mention my trip to the United States Senate. I had a pass to the gallery and while observing a debate, suddenly became overcome with nausea. [This must be an occupational hazard for those who regularly work there.]

A page tried to direct me to the restroom, but I got lost and finally bolted out a side door for some air. I ran directly into the path of Senator Everett Dirksen who was thrown off balance by the impact. Together, we tumbled down half a flight of large concrete steps. Within seconds, the Secret Service was around us. They wanted to detain me, to take me in for questioning. Senator Dirksen demanded to know what for.

"What will the charge be?" he said, "Off-sides? Holding? Unnecessary roughness? If you were smart you'd see if you could act as her agent in a contract with the Green Bay Packers."

They not only let me go but showed me the way to the ladies' room.

These kinds of things have continued to happened to me all my life I am afraid. Fortunately, I have been very lucky and not yet been killed or gone to prison for mugging a Senator. Under the circumstances, however, the thought of a Guardian Angel was certainly a relief to my family.

"Thank God," said my mother, "We finally have someone to keep an eye on you."

Since my Angel's appearance, not a day goes by that I don't think of him, pray for him, and wonder about his message. Especially in the midst of such personal chaos, of the turning over of days and night, events and crises, in a world basically unfit for angels; although one which more than ever before in history would benefit from a divinely illuminating influence, a world in which angels fell disastrously out of favor with the practical philosophic pronouncements of John Locke and his contemporaries, during the Age of Reason. Now, these divine messengers, harbingers of protection and inspiration, are less likely than ever before to be recognized and appreciated. They have been pushed out of our intellectual and spiritual presence to join the ranks of mere supernatural phenomena. Have we forgotten that the difference between this world and the next is but a single breath? A small matter of a veil, a dimensional perception. Nothing really to keep us separated from the all-comprehending angels, unless we want it so in our hearts.

Yet, at the same time, we may as well be divided by galaxies; our worlds could not differ more. And, after my Angel's appearance, over the next few months of legal and personal turmoil, I had a hard time reconciling the presence of a divine being with the ethical and moral circus, the nonsense which transpired with the advent of lawyers in my life.

You see, the first and most critical feature in obtaining a divorce is that each party must have an attorney, and then the attorneys must have lunch. Don't ask me how they can eat at a time like this, but they are extremely hungry, in every sense of the word. Lunch apparently consists of a club sandwich and a couple drinks which cost in the neighborhood of five thousand dollars. Although you are not invited, you pay the check. During this luncheon get together, these gentlemen will decide how they will liquidate most of your assets to cover their fees. Anything that is inadvertently left over, they will recommend you go to court and fight for, all in the spirit of justice.

Subsequent discussions -- in my situation anyway -- were evidently held at a few upper-crust bars, with all the principles except me in attendance, as my fate was decided. At least, I received correspondence to that effect. When my ex-husband's attorney left the courtroom arm-in-arm with the judge, I began to suspect something was amiss. With an IQ somewhere in the triple digits, I could readily recognize the difference between a two-sided negotiation and thinly-veiled assault. And to think: I had initiated the proceedings! I was, in fact, beginning to feel like the javelin thrower who won the coin toss and elected to receive. It is difficult to countenance my Angel putting up with such goings-on. But there you have it.

In essence, this supposed "hearing" removed the last bit of anything which remained to me: my freedom. My lawyer had recommended an all-out job search in the city in order to demonstrate that positions in my field were simply unavailable here, that I should be permitted a wider search for employment.

"This is no time to write a book," he said. "You have to prove you're earnestly looking for a fulltime job and one doesn't exist."

It seemed an incredible waste of time, this business of demonstrating that no jobs existed, especially since that meant once more shelving my plans to write as I did what the lawyer instructed. And dozens of fruitless interviews later, I had amply proved his point. Businesses were cutting back, closing down, not hiring additional executive personnel or writers.

The one and only substantial offer had come as the result of a joke. A friend had goaded me into completing a job application with the federal government and taking an aptitude test to work with the Department of State. The test consisted of questions about international politics, government, geography, world economics, foreign cultures, and language. I had expected to fail miserably and prove his idea completely outrageous. But, in the meantime, having become better friends with Dr. Joan Gilabert who translated my Catalan letter, I had learned a great deal more than I originally planned. Say the words, "United Europe" to Dr. Gilabert and he launches into a four hour presentation of his political and economic philosophy. He is an internationally respected lecturer on these issues and has the flair to prove it. Practically everything he told me over the course of our conversations was on the test. Ultimately, the State Department offered me education in their foreign language school and a position in the diplomatic corps.

However, the contents of my job search file and details of my single job possibility were never admitted as evidence. The judge ultimately signed a decree that, although I was returned to single status, I would never be allowed to move without written permission from my ex-husband or an order of the court. I was a divorced prisoner, and by court mandate, still unemployed, still dependent, in the land of the free and the home of the brave!

Disappointed, angry, embarrassed, chagrined, I wanted to demand of my Angel how he could allow this to happen. Yet, I knew that the power of his appearance had forever changed my father and, because of our closeness, me as well. Deep inside, I believed there had to be a reason I could not leave. But what on earth was it? How would I ever have my own life with attorneys throwing up road blocks everywhere? How would I support myself and my children? I had no interest in a life of dependence. What's more, I was furious to realize I had again put writing aside, wasted all that time, to undertake the fiasco of a worthless job search.

Sifting through the implications of these frustrating events, I gradually came to realize there are two sides to the equation of Truth: being believed and believing. The first is the factual side, the right and wrong dichotomy my mother taught me. You are telling the Truth or you are lying, she would say. There is no middle ground. No such thing as half of the Truth.

"Well?," she would question us, "Is it or isn't it?" And you had better be prepared to discern black from white then and there and stand behind your decision until Hell freezes over. On the matter of Truth my mother was, and is, uncompromising and relentless. This is the part of Truth mothers worry about, the morality that creates forthright people who can be believed. A morality which does not always prevail, even in a court of law, I found.

The other side of Truth, the believing, I learned from a man named John Bryan Diehl. He taught Humanities at our high school and I spent most of every day with him for two years. The school sponsored an experimental learning program for a small group of students; a class which treated literature, linguistics, history, geography, journalism, public speaking, social science, Art and world cultures as one all-encompassing curriculum.

JBD, as we called him, had a unique and exciting teaching method. He allowed students to raise any questions they wished. Sometimes the entire class would address these issues. Sometimes a debate would ensue. But, more often than not he would direct individual students to seek their answers for themselves.

"Go right now and find out!," he would say, handing one of us a pass to the library to spend whatever time was necessary to solve our problem. He would practically push us out the door. When we returned, he would want to know what we had found, what we had learned. Did we think or believe any differently than we had before? This influence of needing to "go right now and find out" has followed me for the rest of my life.

John Diehl's style was unsurpassed for the sense of immediacy it brought to students. When we studied the Constitution, we read it to each other seated in Constitution Hall where the original debates had taken place. We studied world cultures wearing headsets at the United Nations, listening to the discussions of the international representatives. We learned about war standing in front of Picasso's mural "Guernica" in the United Nations' lobby. We discussed George Washington's revolutionary war strategies seated at Fraunce's Tavern in New York City, where he plotted his maneuvers.

John Diehl had a magnificent bass voice and sang professionally with the Moravian Choir, which added all sorts of dimensions to our studies. He played music of all types and from every culture, from the classics to jazz, as a background to his lectures. When we tackled a unit about Africa, he had all of us singing and dancing to the "Missa Lubba" (the Congolese

Mass) and taught Kenyan folk songs he had learned in the Peace Corps.

JBD presented literature to us with unbounded enthusiasm, especially poetry which he seemed to live and breathe as he read it. From him I learned that among the Arts, poetry is the ideal residence for Truth and Belief; an art form in which sound and meaning are skillfully organized to celebrate human understanding. Poetry gives Belief a body, a voice, a reality so that we and the spirit of Truth may walk together and converse. Poetry works its magic on us by means of a musical cadence which open the doors of the heart, allowing the encoded metaphorical message of the poet to find its way directly to the Soul. With poetry it is possible to teach or learn almost anything. And the poetry a person grows to love is his or her individual emotional and spiritual signature, the genetic code of their Soul.

Tell me the poetry you love and I will tell you mine, and we can dispense forever with names, faces, handshakes and greetings. I will know you, recognize you, anywhere; in any remote corner of the world in the darkest night; under blankets of densest fog; in the midst of riots, disasters, chaos and confusion; beyond Death's door. I will know how to find you in an instant and you will know the same of me.

Of all the experiences in the Arts which he imparted to us, I think John Diehl most enjoyed unveiling the works of the great masters. He regularly commandeered a school bus and we descended upon several of the world's greatest museums: the Rodin, the Philadelphia Museum of Art, the Mellon Art Gallery, the Guggenheim. We studied prints and art books for weeks in advance, building expectations about what we would see of the works of Monet, Chagall, Matisse, Rubens, Velasquez, Delacroix, Picasso, Fragonard, Whistler, Rembrandt, VanGogh, Lautrec, Gaughin. We went armed with what we thought to be substantial knowledge. Even carried magnifying glasses to view the diminutiveness of Van Eyck's famous one-hair brush strokes. But the reality of it all swept us away. It was breathtaking, almost unimaginable.

I remember walking through parts of these museums as though I had been there today. I recall standing at the portico of the Philadelphia Museum, with John Diehl explaining how the view down the mall to the city hall building held the wealth of an artistic dynasty of sculptors: the gigantic metal mobile over our heads sculpted by William Calder, the statue of George Washington across the parkway sculpted by Calder's grandfather, the statue of William Penn atop the city hall by his great-grandfather.

I can still feel the sensation of stepping into a gallery that held Fragonard's "The Swing," and standing spellbound before this magnificent larger-than-life painting of a beautiful, elegantly dressed woman on a swing in a bower, laughing, sailing into the treetops with such force of life and reality it seemed she would soon be out of the picture and into the room with us. Most poignantly, I remember first catching sight of Eugene Delacroix's "Algerian Child," a sepia-toned, delicate and mystical portrait of a dark-haired dark-eyed child, the essence of innocence.

These are the experiences of the Truth of Believing, the experience of the Arts within human history. See it. Feel it. Touch it. Sense it. Know it. Capture it. Love it. Remember it. That is what John Diehl taught us.

Besides all of this, John Diehl was the first in my experience to bring up the issues of prejudice, racism, genocide, human versus property rights, and the equality of the sexes. And in formal debates on these kinds of issues, he often made us take the side we did not believe in, so that we had to come to grips with the opposite point of view. JBD was a strong proponent of detailed knowledge and critical thinking. He had a prolific repertoire in many subject areas and no sloppy scholarship was likely to slip by. And, out of everything he taught me, I gradually built a credo for my life. I learned how to investigate, evaluate, and ultimately how to believe: about the Truth of believing. And, in the end, this was the legacy that sustained me.

The factual side of Truth, the right and wrong of morality, had seemed to let me down. I had seen in a courtroom that someone could cheat skillfully and win. Perhaps that is because this variety of Truth has sunk below the level of a spiritual value among us; has come to belong to politics and to the law, and is tinged with a degree of fallibility accordingly.

The Truth of believing and faith, on the other hand, still belongs to God, to Angels, to the eternal Music, to Artists and to Poets. I knew that kind of Truth, in all its magical power, would never betray me. It was oddly more real and absolute than any legal decision, mandate, or rule of order. And that may be enough. For, the Truth of believing may be the only force that really does prevail as the one eternal attainment of this life, the only reality that accompanies us forever. All else fades away.

In coming to this realization, I could see it was time for drastic measures and time to really listen to my Angel, to "go where the music is" as he had told me to in life. By the end of the legal proceedings, my mind was made up.

In his office after the day in court, my attorney said, "So, we'll need your signature on all this in a couple weeks. Where will we reach you?"

"At the opera house," I told him. "I'll give you a phone number when I get one."

"What?" he said.

"The opera," I repeated.

"Oh, yeah," he answered, looking baffled at my response, "You're one of those artsey types. To the opera, huh? What's playing anyway?"

"I am," I said, "Finally!" and left him with his confused thoughts and expression.

Journalist, Bill Moyers, in televised discussions with Professor Joseph Campbell on the subject of "finding your bliss," said that he had the sense of "unseen hands" helping him at different times in his life when he was close to the truth about something, when he was finding his way and seemed to be on the right track. Campbell agreed. He too had had this experience. When he was headed in the right direction, someone always seemed to be there at just the correct moment with the book, thought, or opportunity that he needed. I remember trying to imagine what that must be like. Now I know.

For, as matters legal slid steadily downhill, other illuminating occurrences took precedence, dwarfing the sense I had of being trapped. It all began with a revelation that came as a result of someone lending me a book. Inside was a folded piece of paper which evidently had been used as a bookmark. The paper outlined "The Dynamics of Prayer," a title which caught my attention. This is an interesting and difficult subject for many of us.

Oddly enough, we seem to get into the biggest trouble praying for what we really believe we want. Since we lack important details about the overall scheme of things, what we want and what is best often have nothing in common. We pray for specifics, and when we don't get them we pout. Crying and angry, eyes closed, swearing, we miss the answer entirely, the reply a kindly God lays before us.

Prayer is something so personal that any particular process for prayer is somehow hard to imagine. And yet, that's exactly what the paper I found suggested. The procedure recommended five very specific steps and was an excerpt from the book "Principles of Bahá'í Administration," a publication of the Bahá'í Faith. The guidelines, composed by the Guardian of the Bahá'í Faith, Shoghi Effendi, suggested this method of solving problems and obtaining Divine assistance.

First Step -- Pray and meditate about it. Use the prayers of the Manifestations as they have the greatest power. Then remain in the silence of contemplation for a few minutes.

Second Step -- Arrive at a decision and hold this. This decision is usually born during the contemplation. It may seem almost impossible of accomplishment but if it seems to be an answer to a prayer or a way of solving the problem, then immediately take the next step.

Third Step -- Have determination to carry the decision through. Many fail here. The decision, budding into determination, is blighted and instead becomes a wish or a vague longing. When determination is born, immediately take the next step.

Fourth Step -- Have faith and confidence that the power will flow through you, the right way will appear, the door will open, the right thought, the right message, the right principle or the right book will be given you. Have confidence, and the right things will come to your need. Then, as you rise from prayer, take at once the fifth step.

Fifth Step -- Then, ACT; act as though it had all been answered. Then act with tireless ceaseless energy. And as you act, you, yourself, will become a magnet, which will attract more power to your being, until you become an unobstructed channel for the Divine power to flow through you. Many pray but do not remain for the last half of the first step. Some who meditate arrive at a decision, but fail to hold it. Few have the determination to carry the decision through, still fewer have the confidence that the right thing will come to their need. But how many remember to act as though it had all been answered? How true are those words -- 'Greater than the prayer is the spirit in which it is uttered.' and greater than the way it is uttered is the spirit in which it is carried out.

The day I began this process, I determined to go forward with research for The Book, with or without Mr. Carreras' reply. I could wait no longer for his answer. Hopefully he would catch up later down the road somewhere. And, as I made the decision, almost immediately, I realized a preoccupation I'd developed over a few months that might hold an answer. When the renewal notice had arrived for season tickets to the opera it was obvious that they were unaffordable. With no funds to call my own until the legal process was complete, I had to account for every expenditure as a "necessity." And although they represented the only entertainment I generally purchased all year, opera tickets could hardly be designated a necessity. Besides, these were expensive, wonderful seats in the center of the membership circle, a luxury under any circumstances.

Regardless, the brochure which advertised the new season contained some spectacular art work, especially the illustration for the production of Wagner's "The Valkyrie," ["Die Walküre"] which depicted three wild, blue horses charging down the skies above the glowing eye of a powerful storm. With a magnet, I fastened the brochure to the side of the refrigerator. And every time I passed, gazed again at the picture, thinking how bleak the winter would be with no nights at the opera.

The new process of prayer changed the way I looked at that brochure. Why wasn't it possible to go?, I thought. Just go a different way. I needed information, legitimate language and details to write about opera. If I were allowed to attend rehearsals for the new season I could learn everything I needed about operatic production. With that background, I could write a fictional book to understand the essence of the subject. And, when Mr. Carreras answered me, I would be far ahead of the game in terms of creating his artistic portrait.

In fact, it suddenly occurred to me that, after all the years of fighting schedules and conflicting priorities to find the time to write, there was literally nothing left for me to do but to write. Coming to this realization vastly expanded my view of the future. Everything was beginning to make sense. My Angel obviously had far more intelligence that I. Now I could see why I was stuck here with no job.

The woman who answered the telephone at the Arizona Opera's administrative headquarters told me I would need an appointment with Mr. Glynn Ross, General Director of the company. He would determine whether my request to attend rehearsals could be considered. He saw me at his office a few days later. You will find Glynn Ross listed in the Metropolitan Opera Encyclopedia under "Seattle," the city of his fame. He is the author of the American Bayreuth, the first Wagnerian Festival Opera in the United States. Wagnerian Festivals serve as a mecca for the multitudes of Wagner adherents throughout the world who are devoted to fine performances of the "Ring Cycle," the centerpiece of Wagner's work consisting of a series of four operas which tell the mythological epic story of the struggle between men and the gods for control of the earth. Devotees of the "Ring Cycle" are a select and intellectual group, even among opera goers. And Mr. Ross had produced a festival which held their interest and won their praise. Thank God I didn't know any of this when I went to talk with him. I may have been too intimidated and stayed home. To me, Mr. Ross was a slim, dapper gentleman in a three-piece suit, seventy-ish, with wavy white hair and an intense, but friendly, expression. He gave me the impression he might have x-ray vision; might be reading my mind. We spoke for a few moments about my writing projects.

I could watch him thinking as he rose and said, "Let's go for a walk." We strolled out into the cavernous rehearsal hall.

"You know," he said, "It really doesn't work for anyone to sit in on rehearsals. A production company is a team. If you're not playing, everyone wonders what you're doing there. You're the drop of lemon in the glass of milk."

I could understand how that would be, I told him.

"If you were to be here," he went on, "you would have to be doing something toward the production." We approached the company's grand piano and I commented on its manufacturer. It was a name I didn't know.

"Do you play?" Mr. Ross inquired.

"Yes," I said.

"As an accompanist?" he asked.

"Not for many years," I said.

He explained their accompanist was suffering with tendonitis and might miss the first rehearsals. I assured him that I would need a lot of practice before I would attempt to accompany professional vocalists.

"Do you speak German?" he asked. Their next production would be Wagner's "The Valkyrie," whose advertisement I had admired.

"No," I said. "I studied Latin, Ancient Greek, Spanish, French. Not great credentials for opera, I'm afraid."

We continued walking.

"Did you ever take any theatre arts courses, do you know anything about stage direction or stage management?" he asked.

"No, not that either." My spirits were slowly descending. This was not going to work.

We had circled the entire rehearsal hall and were back to the doors where we had entered. I held out my hand to Mr. Ross to say good-bye.

"Thank you for hearing my ideas," I said. "I have always admired what this company produces, and I wouldn't want to detract from it in any way. Although I'd love to contribute, I just don't see how. Thanks for your time."

A tall, slender dark-haired woman was slowly approaching us from across the hall. She stopped a few feet away and Mr. Ross introduced me to Nina Daldrup, the company's production coordinator.

"Meet Nancy Warren." he said, "She's going to be working with us on "The Valkyrie."

He shot his demand for a commitment back at me, "Right?"

I was stunned, but nodded.

"Nina will give you a vocal score before you leave," he told me. "Study the opera. Rehearsals begin in three weeks."

What had inspired him to let me in? At the time, I couldn't imagine. I still don't know. It was a miracle. But only the first of many.

Chapter Nine

Five hundred years before the birth of Christ, the master philosopher, Pythagorus, developed both the basis for modern mathematics and for Western music. Pythagorus deftly drew the comparisons, schematics of the building blocks, which described the continuity of form between music and science; the threads which wove them together into the fabric of the universe. At that time, and for centuries after, no one would have confused music with entertainment any more than they would have confused science with juggling. These were serious concerns for the theoreticians. Music was not the basis for a Saturday night downtown; science not the means for inventing a new type of engine. Through understanding the conjunction of music with science, the numerical and spiritual codification at the center of existence, scholars hoped to find the key to universal truths and to the purpose of life on earth. No one dreamed that some day the average person might buy a ticket to a musical production or trade the creative fruits of his scientific labors for mere money. Music and science were lofty pursuits and did not figure in the routine material undertakings of society until the time of the Industrial Revolution.

With so many forces opposing its birth, how and why did such an elaborate art form as opera develop during the Sixteenth Century? According to author Jamie James and his recent work, "The Music of the Spheres," opera started as the focus of a purist revival, as the result of Vincenzo Galilei, father of Galileo Galilei, proposing to revive the monody --the single simplistic melodic lines and compositions -- of classic Greek music. Enough of the perversion of polyphony! Galilei wanted something simpler, purer. With the practical and philosophic support of nobleman Giovanni Bardi, the first operas were produced. Bardi's salon, the Camerata, became the home of the first opera company. The original format called for a play interspersed with free-standing vocal works which had nothing to do with the theme of the drama. This was soon adjusted to coordinate the music and theater performance. Gradually, parts of the plays were sung, rapidly evolving into the concept of the musical score and libretto with which we are familiar today.

Paradoxically enough, this attempt at purism, at a return to the simplest forms of music -- the single melodic line sung by a single voice -- heralded the birth of the most complex, voluptuous and sensuous musical art form ever developed: opera. Even among early opera producers, the tendency was toward elaborate costuming and exotic scenery, with ships that sailed across the stage and monsters breathing real flames. Opera has never been a tame sport, even at its inception. It is what Glynn Ross refers to as "the improbable art - the most expensive of the arts - the undeniable empress of the Arts." A very apt description.

Frankly, until I signed on to work with the Arizona Opera, I had never really considered how the complex beauty of an opera is transformed from a musical score and libretto onto a stage. Obviously, someone would have to sing, someone would need to play the music. Beyond that, I had no real concept of the responsibilities of all those other participants listed in the program. What did a stage manager or a stage director do? What was the role of lighting designers, electricians, fly men, carpenters and pin rail specialists in all of this? I was about to find out there is lots more to an operatic production than buying a ticket and showing up on time for the curtain. It should be said, in fact, that opera constitutes a vast area of study. I would never pretend to be expert at any of it. That would require a lifetime on the operatic stage. Nonetheless, by necessity, I learned alot quickly and in the most interesting way possible: as part of a production team.

My education began at a meeting in the opera company's administrative offices immediately after Glynn Ross gave his sanction to my participation in the production of "The Valkyrie." I realized that poor unsuspecting Nina, the production coordinator I'd met for a moment three weeks previously, had the interesting assignment of figuring out what to do with me; with this person who had no staging experience, who didn't speak German, who in fact knew nothing germane to anything that concerned her and her production problems. If she was panicked, it didn't show. She talked about several options.

I could help with logistics, with ferrying performers around, typing schedules, administrative tasks, that sort of thing. Or, she said, I could jump right in as Assistant Stage Director and see if I could manage. I didn't know what any of these might ultimately entail but told her I'd like to do everything that could be fit into a day's work. All of them, if possible.

She looked a little amused at this, but did not discourage me at all, extending an invitation to several auditions, to a meeting of the wardrobe department and to the opening administrative meetings for the current production. As time went on, I realized that the opera company was more than professional enough to absorb the enthusiasm of one bumbling amateur. I learned that, in fact, the calm and clarity that prevails among a professional production staff serves as a stable hub for the entire company, even in the semi-controlled chaos of live performance.

In a final warning, Mr. Ross made it clear that, once rehearsals had begun, everyone's presence was counted on absolutely through the performance schedule; there could be no second thoughts or backing out.

"A lot of this work is hardly glamorous," he told me. "Think it over carefully and if you find you have changed your mind, let me know right away."

Yes, thinking it over certainly would be the sane approach for a rank amateur to take. That sounded reasonable enough. I should certainly consider such a commitment carefully. Yet, once outside the building, reason was nowhere evident.

I jumped into my car, slammed the door and screamed into the windshield, "O My God Almighty! I'm working at the opera!"

At home, the children and my parents were very impressed with my new position...whatever it was. Most others were intrigued but confused about this turn of events. Why do this when you might still be able to find something temporary as a business and technical consultant, most of them questioned? The look in their eyes said, "You were always so down to earth and logical. Have you flipped your lid?" Oh well, I probably had, but the illogic and excitement of it carried that day and many to follow.

December had rolled around and Christmas loomed just ahead. This year, for the first time in my life, the holidays had been more of a hurdle and a struggle than a pleasure. The last throes of the legal proceedings made everything more difficult and life in general more tentative. On Christmas Eve, the judge, in his innate wisdom, finalized our divorce decree. I was called by the attorney's office to sign and pick up the papers and returned home just in time to see my two little ones off for their first holiday ever away from home.

Daniel had come down with a cold and seemed to be feverish. He was fighting tears. Adrienne's wide eyes attested to her confusion and uncertainty about this strange turn of events. It was the hardest thing I had ever done to put them into their father's car and say good-bye. I watched them drive away until the tail lights disappeared around the bend in the road, then leaned against the garden wall and cried a whole year's agony into the cold cement.

What had I done? I had turned life upside down, torn up and destroyed any sense of order and tradition our family had ever had. And for what? I had relinquished my job, most ties of friendship, our home, my freedom, financial stability, even holidays with my children. Was I crazy?

Take Halloween as a symptom of this schizophrenia. I had gotten the usual exotic costumes together: the Phantom of the Opera for Daniel, a fuzzy rabbit suit for Adrienne, and the Grim Reaper for Rachel. And when I reached for the camera -- no film! There would be no pictures of this year's costumes; a first ever failure on my part. Typical of my scatterbrained, lackluster performance these days. The most basic details were forgotten, ruining everything. I cried harder, furious with myself. By then, tears had soaked through the arms of my jacket and I began searching pockets for a handkerchief.

A small voice behind me stopped my searching. "Nancy?"

It was Helen, who lived on the hill across the way. She offered me a handkerchief. She and her husband, Chuck, the retired owners of a nursery school, especially liked my children, watching over them while they played outside, sending them special treats and gifts. Helen had evidently witnessed the children's departure.

"You know," she said, "Chuck and I were both divorced before we married. We think you've done the right thing. Don't worry so much about the children. They take good care of each other. And it takes time to adjust."

Although I kept right on crying, her certainty gave me more confidence in the path I had chosen. Then she did something amazing.

"Here," she said, "I think you need these more than I do." And, she handed me pictures she had taken at their front door of the children in their Halloween costumes.

I think every hair on my head stood on end. It was uncanny. She could not have known the specific subject of the lecture I'd just given myself. How could she have thought to hand me those pictures at that particular moment? The tears shut off. I would take her word for it. Everything would be fine.

And, more and more, everything was. My sole misgiving about going to work at the opera was that financially, it only reimbursed work-related expenses. Besides, I couldn't even be positive of the outcome of my efforts there; had no assurance that I would be making strides toward writing something fit for publication. Meanwhile, finances would continue to be tight until the property settlement was concluded. A guilty little voice in the back of my mind said I should be continuing to search for the nonexistent job, just because anything else constituted laziness. Shouldn't I at least try to plan for emergencies if they arose?

But, when problems did arise, the issue of money proved superfluous and I was glad I had gone after my dream instead of focusing on my bank account. For, almost from the moment I began work at the opera, help to take care of everything else started arriving out of nowhere. Rehearsals began at ten o'clock in the morning and often ran until ten o'clock at night. Just the issue of childcare loomed large. Rachel generously volunteered to give up her own plans to take care of the two little children after school. A friend of Rachel's, the son of a caterer, insisted on coming by every night of rehearsals and cooking meals.

"No problem," he said. He was practicing to open his own restaurant.

When the yard and garden began to look shabby from lack of attention, a gardener friend who "Just happened to be in the neighborhood," (he lives on the other side of the city) spent an entire day putting it to rights. He refused to take anything for his trouble. The day our outdoor lamp post gave up the ghost, a neighbor known by one and all as the village grump, was spotted by my children kindly dismantling and fixing the light for us.

I was panicked when the lawn sprinkler system exploded. This constituted major havoc. Here it seemed I might be up against a situation nobody would magically "bail me out of." I was wrong. I picked the name of an irrigation company from among several dozen advertisements in the telephone directory. The new proprietor, it turned out, had done yard work for me two years before. Did I remember, he asked, that his son had been having alot of problems when he last saw me?

"Yes," I said.

"Do you remember the advice you gave me?" he asked.

I did not.

"Well, I do, and I always wanted to thank you, because your advice worked. My son is doing fine now," he said. "Let me fix the sprinkler system for you. No charge. It means alot to me to do something in return."

I honestly could not remember having said anything so impressive or wonderful. But this friend I hadn't known I had insisted on spending the next day fixing the several geysers in our yard.

Equally incredible was the attorney friend who called in all sorts of "chips" and professional favors to defray a major portion of my legal expense. He never said what inspired him to do this. He never explained.

The list of helpful friends, neighbors and acquaintances went on and on. Could all of this activity on my behalf be part of the "unseen hands" Bill Moyers and Joseph Campbell were talking about? Whatever it was, I came to the conclusion that some force was definitely in my corner giving me every encouragement to pursue my dream. And, at the very least, I am sure that, from the day I stepped into the opera office, The Uninvited Guest stood staunchly at one side, my Guardian Angel at the other. I have had a lot of help.

And certainly, the moral support never hurt a bit. During the three weeks that I had waited for rehearsals to begin, there had been plenty of time for second thoughts to set in.

What if I couldn't do what they expected? What if I turned out to be a liability to the company? As Nina Daldrup had explained more about this particular opera, I became increasingly nervous. In the first place, production of "The Valkyrie," would constitute the first step in establishing a new American Bayreuth. Glynn Ross had determined that he would reproduce his success with the Wagnerian Festival in Seattle by opening one in Arizona. He would start with the production of "The Valkyrie" and build from there, in subsequent seasons undertaking "Siegfried," "Das Rheingold," and "Götterdämmerung," bringing the entire festival into operation by the summer of 1996. At the festival, these operas would be performed consecutively over a period of several days in a theatre yet to be chosen -- hopefully near the Grand Canyon -- creating an unbeatable tourist attraction of natural spectacle and operatic performance which would draw visitors from around the world. Funding for the future festival was dependent upon the success of this production of the "The Valkyrie," I was told.

Upon learning that Maestro Henry Holt would conduct, my sense of intimidation grew. A native of Vienna and a product of its famed music culture, Henry is renowned for his successes as the conductor of more Wagnerian opera than anyone else in North America. Besides a prolific career as a conductor in the United States and Canada, he had helped to build the Seattle festival as its resident music director. He would not only conduct, but also serve as artistic director, taking charge of the overall interpretation. The artistic approach would be relatively traditional, despite a sparse, abstract set (dominated by a slanted platform or "rake" with several sets of stairs), scenic backdrops which were projected onto a screen behind the rake, and minimal use of stage furniture and handprops. As a native Austrian, Henry was very proficient in the German language as well as in English and provided any "judgment calls" in translations for the production.

My immediate supervisor, Claus Koenig, would perform the role of stage director. He hailed from Munich, Germany, where he grew up steeped in the tradition of Wagnerian Opera. Although still quite young for his position, he had already paid his dues as assistant director, at the Bavarian State Opera and Munich National Theater, where he was a protege of the late Jean Pierre Ponelle, legendary stage director of European opera. Claus' responsibility was for the dramatic interpretation, the characterization given to each role, as well as the consistency of stage action with the musical intent of the composer.

Visually, center stage for this production would go to the costuming, minutely detailed creations of fantasy which were the creative effort of famed designer, Peter J. Hall. The sketchboard drawings alone amounted to works of art. These were translated into reality by Wardrobe Manager, Gio Ross, and the costume department. Gio is Glynn Ross's wife and a mainstay of this company as well as those he has led in the past.

Having acquired a full understanding of the scope and professional quality of this project, I seriously thought about bowing out. However, The Uninvited Guest was in top form that week and wouldn't hear of it. So, instead I decided to get to the rehearsal hall early to set up everything as Mr. Ross had instructed. Even so, I was unprepared for my first meeting with Claus. I had planned a no-nonsense professional greeting that would instill plenty of confidence (hopefully in me as well) that I knew what I was doing.

Claus, a tall, thin man with dark curly hair and black-rimmed glasses, walked up and shook my hand, looking at me intently, "So, I'm glad we work together here. You have nice eyes," he said with overtones of a heavy German accent.

So much for my impressive professional greeting. I could think of no response. What was the point in such a comment anyway? Was he one of these men who reduce women to a list of physical attributes to keep them in their place? How should I

116

reply? But he had moved on immediately, greeting the performers, and wasn't waiting for my answer. Later, I was glad I said nothing, because I had totally misread his intention. Claus is part professional stage director, part professional child. And within the child resides the true genius. He does not have to unlearn the stifling habits of the average adult in order to create. Nobody ever trained the spontaneity out of him; nobody ever convinced him to say things he doesn't mean or not say the things he does. So, he tells you what he thinks, which is generally something supportive, complimentary, and kind; and certainly never domineering or condescending. Within a few days, I had a context for his comment. He notices peoples' strengths -- physical, artistic, intellectual -- and announces them out loud. He looks at every human being as though he is in the process of placing them on stage and lighting their features to the best advantage.

"And now, we all get to work," Claus announced. He turned to me. "I want you to record all the entrances, exits, crosses, any important staging cues. We're using American, not European left and right stage directions. OK?"

Was he speaking English or German, I wondered? Should I be blunt and tell him I didn't have a foggy clue what he was talking about?

Claus smiled at my perplexed expression. "You know, I don't expect an assistant to spend the rest of their life getting coffee for everybody," he said. "I don't want to bore you. Take charge on whatever you are able and really learn this."

Coffee. Yes, there was a word I recognized. Cream and sugar I could understand. The rest of his instructions were a meaningless blur. I quietly asked him for a private word at one side of the rehearsal hall and took a deep breath before posing my question. Now they would ask me to leave, I thought.

"Would you mind explaining what you're talking about?" I asked him. "I have no idea what an assistant director does."

Claus never blinked. On the first page of my score he quickly penciled a string of several dozen hieroglyphics, naming them as he wrote. These were abbreviations to describe the action on the stage. I was to keep track of all that went on "of any significance." Don't worry about the details, he said, singers change those all the time and that's fine.

"Everybody develops their own system for keeping notes," he said. "There's no right or wrong way."

He instructed me to add any other references I felt we needed and discuss them with him later. Start with this responsibility, he said, we would add others as we went along. He clapped his hands and rehearsal began. My God, I said to myself, he was going to expect me to know how to do this? I hoped we didn't end up with instructions for a burlesque show instead of an opera.

Ultimately, however, my fears were unfounded. With the rehearsal underway, everything fell into place and made perfect sense. Within a few days, I found I could keep, not only Claus's notes, but notes to the individual singers' specifications as well, comparing scores after rehearsals so that they could copy references to any details they wanted to remember. To my astonishment, everything about the process of staging seemed as natural to me as breathing. Soon I could focus most of my attention away from the mechanics and onto the deeper meaning, the dramatic core, of the production.

It is difficult at best to get the sense of an opera from reading a libretto, or even a condensed story line. But, briefly, for those unfamiliar with "The Valkryie," this story explains the plight of Siegmund, son of the god, Wotan, and a mortal woman. Siegmund has lost home and family to plunderers and is unaware of his father's identity. His weapons were destroyed defending a helpless woman and he stumbles exhausted into the home of the villainous Hunding. He is welcomed by Hunding's wife, Sieglinde. They sense some sort of bond between them and, when Hunding challenges Siegmund to combat, Sieglinde drugs her husband's drink so that she can speak to Siegmund alone. She offers him a weapon, a powerful sword driven into a stump by a cloaked stranger: Wotan. They realize they are brother and sister; that they are in love. Drawing the sword, Siegmund promises to flee with Sieglinde.

Wotan favors Siegmund in the battle and sends Brunnhilde, his favorite of nine daughters (the Valkyries), to protect his son.

But his plan is overruled by Fricka, his wife. She says Sieglinde and Siegmund have defiled the sanctity of marriage and must be punished. Wotan eventually accedes to her and recalls Brunnhilde. Brunnhilde attempts to warn Siegmund and, tracking down the couple in their flight, promises to take him to Valhalla. He will not leave Sieglinde's side and Brunnhilde pities him, impressed by their bond of human love. She decides to champion him.

During the combat of Siegmund and Hunding, Wotan appears, overriding Brunnhilde's protection of Siegmund, shattering the magic sword, then contemptuously killing Hunding who has murdered Siegmund. Brunnhilde flees with Sieglinde who has realized she is expecting Siegmund's child. Brunnhilde begs her sister Valkyries to shield them from Wotan, which they attempt, but soon find they are not strong enough to withstand his wrath. Wotan determines he must punish Brunnhilde by condemning her to mortality, then, overcome with her pleas and with his paternal emotions, determines with Brunnhilde that, although mortal, she will be eternally encircled by a magic ring of fire until the kiss of a hero releases her.

This is an extremely difficult opera to stage. Four hours in length, it consists of many long scenes and passages dedicated to Wagner's elaborate, winding melodies and to vocal exchanges between only two or three characters. Nonetheless, I came to resent the assertions I have heard that Wagner is tedious and not melodic, that his music is too complex, his topics too weighty, to be familiar or appealing.

I remembered an explanation of Wagner's melodic nature from Leonard Bernstein's "Young People's Concert" series that I had seen as a child and did a little research to refresh my memory. Bernstein had said, "Certain people find Wagner's operas unmelodic. This is why: because Wagner usually constructed those huge operas of his out of tiny little motives, instead of writing regular tunes such as the Italian opera composers used. But how wrong they are to say that Wagner doesn't write melody! He writes nothing but melody!" A motive is a phrase, a mini-melody created out of three or four notes. Bernstein showed how the composer strung these together, overlapped them, to create phrases and underlying harmonies. Out of these miniature phrases, Wagner constructed continuous, passionate melodies enduring ten minutes or longer. The example Bernstein used was the Prelude to "Tristan and Isolde."

To me, the heroic figure in "Valkyrie" is the character Brunnhilde. It is she who has the courage to leap the chasm between the worlds of the gods and human beings. Appropriately, the woman who plays Brunnhilde in such a production must be a larger-than-life personality herself, a soprano with a formidable voice and stage presence, and a penetrating gaze, one of those people you identify immediately as a powerful individual, someone to be reckoned with.

Our soprano, Karen Bureau, was no exception, as a principal performer on contract for several years to the Wagnerian festival of the Hannover Opera in Germany. Apart from Wagnerian roles, she easily managed some of the heaviest female lead roles in opera -- Leonore in "Fidelio," Electra in "Idomeneo," Madeleine in "Andrea Chenier," among them -- in opera houses throughout the world. I later learned that Henry Holt had gone to great lengths to bring her to the United States for this production.

Having been told I was added to the opera staff at the last moment and on a temporary basis, she wanted to know what I hoped to accomplish working as an Assistant Director. I explained about the fictional book as a preliminary step in writing about Carreras, watching her intense blue eyes for a reaction to my unusual purpose.

"You want to write about Carreras, write about him," she said. "Why bother with this other book? Do what you want to do."

I could see she was not only seriously interested but encouraging. She wanted to know why I had been unable to contact Carreras and I explained.

"You're going about this all wrong," she told me. "You need to talk to his management on the telephone or to find out where he is and contact him directly." She was quite clear that my reticence in this regard would never do.

Karen instructed me to go into the office and find several reference books and trade magazines that would list where Carreras would be performing in the future as well as telephone numbers and addresses for his agents.

"You have to figure out how to be in the right place at the right time, that's all," she said.

And, she explained why she had good reason to believe this.

She had gone to work for the Metropolitan Opera in their office to observe, plan, and be available when the right audition came along. When it did, she gave a performance that launched her professional career.

"Find out where he is and call him," she commanded me. "Why wait?"

"What makes you think he will talk to me?" I asked.

"Because I have met him a few times," she said. "And he is very approachable, a really decent person, and will be interested in what you have to say. And when Carreras meets you, he's going to be glad he did."

I noticed her phrasing: "When Carreras meets you" not "if." The winning attitude of the confident principal performer: no tentative or apologetic words, an absolute, a definite, approach to life.

The rehearsal was over and I strolled into the office to look for the references she recommended. Half of me said this was a wonderful new idea and high time I developed a more winning and center-stage attitude. The other half of me said, "Why get so invested in this again? Why invite more disappointment?" Things were going well. I was content with the idea of writing fiction; satisfied not to base my future plans upon a collaboration with Mr. Carreras, a possibility I could not control. Why stir the pot again, creating expectations and turmoil that would probably produce no results?

Not noticing any magazines or entertainment guides on the shelves, I decided to accept that as an omen. As quickly as I'd followed her suggestion, I'd discarded it. There were no answers strewn in my path, so forget it.

But, Karen was right behind me.

"Did you find them?" she asked.

And, in giant steps immediately behind her followed a broad-shouldered six and a half foot tall bass vocalist, Noel Mangin, who sang the part of Hunding, the villain. Noel is world famous as an interpreter of this role, and holds the distinction of singing all the bass roles within a consecutive "Ring" cycle. He had won awards as Knight of the Order of the British Empire and German Kammersanger. And no wonder. His voice is astonishing. So clear and resounding, in fact, that although the stage director arranged to hang a microphone for one production in Seattle in which Noel was to sing from within the depths of a cave, everyone was astounded to find he didn't need it. He projected through the cave walls into the house effortlessly.

And now, I heard that famous voice bellow, "What are you looking for, you two?" Karen explained our search.

"The ladies had them out at the wardrobe department," he announced in his rumbling Australian drawl.

"Well, forget it then," I said. "All the lights are out back there and I don't know where the switches are."

Karen took hold of my arm. "Come on!" she said. "You're not getting anywhere standing here." And she hurried me down the hall to the wardrobe area. I could have sworn I heard the Uninvited Guest laughing.

As I had expected, the room was strange and spooky in the dark. I could see nothing except the eerie shapes of mannequins, the disembodied styrofoam heads which held wigs of all lengths and descriptions. We would find nothing groping around this wax museum, I thought. But there in a beam of moonlight on the cutting table sat the books we sought. Karen snatched them up and back down the hall we tore into the light.

Outside the building, she loaded my arms with the reference manuals.

"Now take these home and read them and start calling," she said. "Let me know how it's going."

The next day, based upon the information I uncovered in the Musical America guide, I spoke to an agency which represented Mr. Carreras in New York. They directed me to his American publicist, Candice Flores, who tried very hard to be helpful with the little information she had.

I was about to hang up from a conversation with her when she suddenly exclaimed, "Oh wait! Here's a circular from London. He'll be there on January 25th for two weeks." And she gave me the telephone number at Covent Garden Opera House.

The number lay on the kitchen counter for several days. Until, one night after rehearsal I made the effort to calculate the time difference between Tucson and London.

It's difficult settling down after a full day of rehearsals. The music and the energy just refuse to subside for quite a while. Everyone develops some method for unwinding. I generally cook supper, play the piano, and then find some task around the house to wear myself out. About two o'clock in the morning, in the midst of taking down Christmas decorations, I realized it would be just past nine a.m. in London. I gave Covent Garden administrative offices a call.

"What are you doing out of bed?" the man who answered the telephone wanted to know. I could tell by the way he said it he mistook my voice for a child calling London without parental permission.

"I'm a writer -- a grownup," I told him. "I'd like to know whether it will be possible to talk with José Carreras about a project proposal when he performs there this month."

"Certainly," he told me. He calculated the date and time I should call and that was that.

I hung up in a daze. You mean it was so easy? Why hadn't I done this a year ago? The next morning, I told Karen who was nearly as thrilled as I was.

"We'll talk later about what to say when you get through to him," she promised.

There was that word again: "when." I hoped it was all so simple as she thought. Two weeks of waiting loomed ahead and, fortunately, I would be too busy to worry inordinately about the outcome. Because, meanwhile, a blistering rehearsal schedule sailed forward; a schedule in which I was so involved that Nina

123

called me into her office for a chat. She was concerned and made no excuses about it.

"Claus relies on you absolutely," she said. "I never expected your job to turn into twelve and fourteen hour days. Are you sure you're going to make it through this?"

It was true. I had all the production notes and blocking. Claus had long since stopped copying any of it into his score. If things got off track in rehearsal, he expected me to say something. Besides that, I had detailed lists of stage management information, memoranda for the wardrobe supervisor and props master, notes for the stage crew and lighting designer. I felt complimented that Claus recognized this was no game, no mere diversion, for me. He took me seriously, trusted me. I would never let him down. I would be there, I assured Nina, short of being hit by a freight train. Nothing could keep me away. I had never had such a wonderful experience before in life. In Pablo Casals' words, "This is supreme." Because we had become a team; synchronized in our efforts. It was an unparalleled feeling to be completely sure how to support someone's creative inspiration that way, to understand exactly where they were headed and why.

Throughout the ups and downs of seemingly endless marathon days, I gradually discovered that, although his professional experience far outweighed mine, Claus and I loved and appreciated opera in a very similar way. In fact, we shared the same worries about the production and the same sleepless nights.

Mr. Ross commented, "It's part of the routine. Unless the directors miss at least three night's of sleep, the production will be no good." In that case, our "Valkyries" must have been a masterpiece.

Of the impressive repertoire of directorial technique of which Claus is capable, I most enjoyed listening to his talks with the performers as he helped the vocalists bring their characters to life. Of course, each singer came prepared with a concept of the role they would perform. Some had sung the part many times, others were making their debut. But no one came armed with such a complete understanding of these characters as Claus did.

He knew their family history, psychological motives, emotional make-up, social customs, spiritual values. He seemed sure of what they had for breakfast. As he and the performers built layers of meaning to these roles -- the nuances of inflection, the emotions, the interactions, the gestures -- I began to understand this art of stage direction and the variations in depth that are possible in operatic performance.

Claus was expert in another feature of production I had never understood as particularly important: lighting. Although I could contribute little, I sat entranced at the elevated lighting table in the center of the music hall for three days observing everything I could about the art of stage lighting. With illumination and color, Claus and lighting designer, Russell Stagg, created moods of sympathy, fury, triumph, fear, and despair, the essence of moonlight seduction, the warmth and fragility of Spring. I had never fully considered the effect that lighting has on the meaning of a performance. As much as any of the words; as much as the music itself. Despite our auditory senses, we are very much visual creatures.

Within three exhilarating weeks, we had been through the entire production process: from the initial piano run-through with individual performers, to the staging and blocking, to the sitzprobe when orchestra meets performers and all the musical elements are combined. We had constructed the lighting and staging cues, worked out all the kinks with costuming, makeup and props, run through two dress rehearsals, settled the issues of onstage electrical requirements, tested the smoke effects which would dramatize Brunnhilde's condemnation to a ring of fire. And, in between, we had dealt with the routine problems of scheduling, accommodations, logistics, chauffeuring, illness and a couple personality conflicts. By opening night, it seemed I had known Claus Koenig and Henry Holt, Glynn and Gio Ross, and Nina Daldrup much longer than a mere month.

Now it was time to turn the production over to the conductor's baton, over to the stage crew who would handle the props, curtains, special effects, and scenery; over to the stage manager who would direct the performance activities, call the entrances, exits, sound effect and lighting cues. Nina asked if I would like tickets for opening night and I gladly accepted for my parents and children. But, there was no way I could sit in the audience. I asked to be backstage, somewhere that I could see exactly what was going on and why.

For, after such an intense effort, when performers walk onto a stage, it is as though you are sending your own children out to perform. In essence, everything that happens to the performers happens to you. If they trip, something inside you falls. If they miss a cue, your heart stops. Trying to act like a normal theater-goer, to relax and enjoy the performance, would be impossible. I most likely would have been standing in my chair; shredding the upholstery off the seat. No, I wouldn't dare sit in the audience.

Thank heaven that, with so much riding on its success, opening night proved to be an overwhelming victory for the performers, for Glynn Ross, for Henry and Claus, for Richard Wagner. An appreciative audience gave all of them a standing ovation and I was happy to join in. As I stood there, basking in the emotion of the moment, in the triumph of these people I so admired, a golden warmth began to fill every cell, from my toes to the roots of my hair. I felt I must be glowing, radiating the light of happiness for all the world to see. I had found my bliss. I was finally home and content, in the society of these artists, in the familiar and comforting company of those I could completely understand.

Together, we had made people applaud, smile, think. For a few hours, we had lifted them out of their everyday existence and shown them something extraordinary, challenging, uplifting. We had given them a few memorable moments of beauty, a few golden coins from the wealth of the Arts, to save for themselves or spend on others as they pleased. I felt like a yacht builder whose boat won the World Cup; a NASA engineer whose rocket touched down safely on the Moon; a scientist who discovered the cure for unhappiness. And for the future, I would have all of this experience to add to the impact of writing, to this book which waited to be produced. What's more, having found an artistic homeland, I had gained a sense of stability, the confidence to go ahead.

"Well God," I whispered under my breath, "With the note you gave me so long ago, I believe I have finally found my melody. And I am very grateful. But please, if it's not too much trouble, just one last favor. May I have five minutes to explain to Mr. Carreras, to find the words to this song and a way to sing this for you...for everyone?"

It may have been the roar of the crowd, but, if God answered, I could not hear Him.

Chapter Ten

"PRESS ON"

Nothing in the world can take the place of persistence. Talent will not; nothing is more common than unsuccessful men with talent. Genius will not; unrewarded genius is almost a proverb. Education will not; the world is full of educated derelicts. Persistence and determination alone are omnipotent.

A proverb Glynn Ross posted over the entrance of the Arizona Opera rehearsal hall.

Only one hour remained until the scheduled call to Covent Garden. I sat next to the kitchen telephone practicing my conversation with Carreras and, when the phone rang, jumped straight into the air. Karen Bureau was calling from the airport on her return trip to Germany. She wanted to offer last minute advice: be confident, be clear, be concise, be friendly, be professional. Karen was, above all, completely supportive. She had an instinct about this project, she said. This was a dream I must somehow realize. And she took time to add to the inspiration, to encourage me not to lose heart halfway through the journey. For the odyssey was not nearly over.

"Now remember," she joked, "When you and José Carreras get to be good friends, tell him I'll be happy to sing 'Andrea Chenier' with him any time." Then serious once more, "Really, when you get through you're going to make a great impression. Trust me."

And why not trust her? She could not know, of course, that she addressed a woman who was used to the presence of Uninvited Guests and Angels, who held impassioned

129

conversations with tangelo trees and sailed gleefully off cliffs into the sea. Trust her? That was a walk in the park compared with other events of the past couple years.

Moments later, trying hard to control my trembling voice, I placed the call to London and was transferred backstage in seconds. The man who answered there, Sandy, was responsible for switching calls to the dressing rooms.

"You want who?," he said in an irritated voice, "They have no right to put your call through. What do they think they're doing? No, of course you can't talk to Mr. Carreras!"

The sudden change in the wind took me off guard. Momentarily, I could think of no response. What would Karen have done? I couldn't imagine. Sadly, I had adopted her approach without the requisite confidence and flair to carry it off. In the end, all I could be was myself,

"Well, are you still there?" the man in London asked.

"Yes," I answered. "Listen, I'm not trying to bother anybody. If this is an inappropriate phone call, I'm sorry. I'm a writer trying to present a proposal for a book project. I have been trying for two years to contact Mr. Carreras' manager through the mail with no response. His American publicist suggested this as an alternate route. Obviously, that was a mistake."

"Just understand," he said, still stiff and officious, "A lot of nuts call here looking for performers."

With that, the temperature on my end of the phone rose. I was starting to boil.

"Well, you just understand," I said, "I'm not one of them. And from the little bit I do know of Mr. Carreras, I don't think he would appreciate being represented by that attitude and tone of voice."

Suddenly, the tone changed. "Maybe I can take a message for you," Sandy said.

I tried explaining the book idea a little bit. Gave him an address and telephone number.

"I'm sorry about putting you through an interrogation," he said, "But that's my job. I'll try to help, but it may take a few calls to get through." He would deliver my message to Fritz

Krammer, Mr. Carreras' secretary, Sandy promised. If I called back on Saturday maybe he could put my call through.

Saturday at Covent Garden was evidently a madhouse. Sandy suggested I send a facsimile of my book proposal through the office. He would deliver that as well. Call back Tuesday, he told me. Tuesday's hurdle turned out to be an early make-up call for Mr. Carreras for a television appearance. A fellow named Mark was on duty backstage that evening. He had been briefed by Sandy.

"Well, you're lucky it's José Carreras you want to talk with," he told me, "and not some snob. He's very friendly. When he comes through here he stops to chat with us."

Great, I reflected, maybe I should stop worrying about learning stage direction and get a job in the security force at Covent Garden. Much to his credit, Mark managed to get so far as to speak simultaneously on two telephones -- with Carreras' secretary, Fritz Krammer, and me.

"It is inconvenient to talk," Mr. Krammer said.

"Mark, please ask if they are interested in book proposals," I said. "Shall I bother to keep trying? If he says there is no point, at least I can forget about it."

I heard Mark deliver my message on the other telephone. He returned.

"It is inconvenient to talk now," he said. "That's all he can tell me. You might try calling the opera's administrative office during their hours, sometimes Fritz stops by there."

But, Mark had no idea what time. It was a shot in the dark, and an expensive one at that. This, like everything else I had attempted, was getting nowhere. And somehow this sense of being so close to explaining my idea and still failing was worse than the silence of unanswered letters and the run-around from New York agents.

In contrast, the experience of "The Valkyrie" had left me feeling so buoyant and exhilarated, so fulfilled and inspired. I wanted that emotion back. No more of this silliness, chasing shadows. I decided to sit down and begin writing the book, with or without the permission of its protagonist. I would write what I knew, what had happened; explain why this book had any relevance in the scheme of things. Four chapters later, I had yet to say anything substantial in explanation of Mr. Carreras' background or his stature as an artist. Now what? I was wandering in a mental wasteland, had lost my sense of direction. And I was homesick for the opera.

Mr. Ross had warned me this would happen. When we moved production of "The Valkyrie," to the Music Hall for dress rehearsals he was in and out of the auditorium throughout the day and evening, checking on progress. Always, at any hour, he ran into me.

Finally, he said, holding up a warning hand, "I hope you realize, there are some people who get a whiff of staging opera and are hooked. It becomes a lifetime addiction, an obsession. And I just have this feeling about you..."

When "The Valkyrie" closed, I had stopped by his office to turn in my score and say good-bye.

"If I can work it out, may I come back to finish the Wagner Festival?" I asked. He smiled and took my hands.

"The candle is always in the window," he said.

Two weeks had transpired since the close of "The Valkyrie." The company was beginning production of "La Boheme." Maybe they could use some help. I gave Nina, the production coordinator, a call and she gladly accepted the offer, assigning me to transport artists from the airport and extending an invitation to sit in on rehearsals.

It was a small involvement, really, but a tie to my inspiration all the same. I had always enjoyed talking to the singers. This might get me back on track. No more Mr. Carreras for the time being, no more Covent Garden, no more pressure to talk to people who wouldn't talk to me. At the airport, Joseph Wolverton, the tenor who was to sing the part of Rodolfo, noticed the "Arizona Opera," sign I held up right away. He was an extremely pleasant person and, loading his luggage into the car, we immediately struck up a conversation. What a relief, I thought, someone who knows nothing of "The Book," and the search for José Carreras. I could start fresh and forget all that for a while.

"So," I said. "Where are you flying in from?"

"Spain," Joseph told me, "I just finished a production of "La Boheme" at the Liceo in Barcelona."

Oh, my God, the ghosts were after me. Barcelona? Carreras' birthplace, hometown, his operatic stomping grounds! Just let it go by!, I told myself. Keep your mouth shut! But, it was like a reflex.

"Really?," I said. "You didn't happen to run into José Carreras did you?" Why had I said it, even in jest? It was the end of peace of mind.

"You like Carreras?" Joseph wanted to know.

Oh, in a way, I told him.

"He was a hero of mine at City Opera," he said.

And we were off. The conversation ended with him promising me copies of his personal tape library of rehearsals and programs featuring Carreras.

I returned to the airport to pick up Jonathon Field, the incoming stage director, the resident stage director of the Chicago Lyric Opera. He should have some fascinating experiences to discuss. So, that's enough, I told myself. No more talk about Carreras. You'll never clear your head that way. Talk about anything else. Mr. Field's' method of stage direction. The weather. The scenery. Politics. The economy.

Jonathon Field was a no-nonsense businesslike person. I could see I'd have no problem sticking to a factual line of conversation. He mentioned he was actually flying into Tucson for the second time that week. He had to rush home due to a death in the family, that of his father in law. I expressed my condolences.

"I'm very lucky to have my parents here with me," I said. "I really don't know what I would do without all their help and backup."

"You are lucky," he assured me. His own father, he said, was quite far away and they rarely saw each other. He was retired and it was a long plane flight to visit him.

"Oh, does he live in Florida?" I asked.

"No," he said. "Actually he lives in Barcelona."

Oh, hell. I thought about stopping the car and throwing him out.

No. I would be quiet. I would say nothing. For once in my life I wouldn't ask.

I asked.

Carreras? No, he told me, he had never met him or seen him perform, not in Barcelona or anywhere else. Why did I want to know?

Without getting too detailed, I explained the project I had been pursuing. There's only one word for the look Jonathon Field gave me: pitying.

"Well," he said, "I hate to be the one to tell you, but your letters might as well be thrown in the ocean. If they were even delivered, no one is going to answer them."

He described the gigantic administrative organizations which surround operatic personalities. I would never get through, he promised, never make a dent or any semblance of an impact. Write about something or someone else. I was wasting my time.

Delivering Jonathon Field at the rehearsal hall, I went looking for Mr. Ross. He spotted me through the cafe scenery of the "La Boheme" set and called out, "Are you alright?"

I must have looked pathetic. "No," I said. "I'm not. Talk to me." And he did.

"Your problem," he said, "Is that you have no bottom line. You can't present a proposal to anybody unless you know what they're going to get out of it. You need a publisher."

Thank God. Was that all? A publisher. Of course. I would get one right away.

Perusing a reference directory, I found a substantial publisher of inspirational books right in Tucson. The director of project development expressed immediate interest, saying I should memorialize my proposal to her in writing and could explain to Mr. Carreras' agents we were discussing details of a publication contract.

Back at Covent Garden, Sandy took delivery of one more FAX letter from me to Fritz Krammer.

"Fritz already told me he will answer you," Sandy said, "After the close of this run of 'Stiffelio.' He's a decent man. If I were you, I'd believe him."

Trusting, faith, confidence, believing. I had spent two years with nothing else on my side. Trusting people I didn't know. Having faith in angels, mysteries and shadows. Believing in forces I couldn't see. If it was a joke, it had grown to such proportions that when the world began to laugh the reverberation would soar right off the Richter Scale.

"Good-bye and thanks for all your help," I told Sandy. "When the book is published, I'll send autographed copies to you and Mark."

Trusting, faith, confidence and believing are the basis for Persistence, that irreplaceable quality referenced by Mr. Ross's sign over the rehearsal hall doorway. It was only when my faith waivered that persistence dimmed. How could I keep these fluctuations in belief from slowing, maybe even halting, progress? I seemed to create my own crises, then try to find ways to rise to these occasions, taking them as seriously as life and death battles. There had to be a means of not living each day like a human yo-yo, emotionally vulnerable to every small twist of fate. These vicissitudes must be brought under some control or this odyssey would become psychologically unendurable. Besides, I might not be so fortunate as to continue meeting people like Karen who would offer so much unsolicited encouragement when my emotions had hit bottom.

The quality which ultimately sustains faith is receptiveness. There lies the key to maintaining continued trust and faith: openness to whatever events transpire. Not to look on each day, each occurrence, as something to be survived in anticipation of the real destination; but to appreciate the entire journey, to notice and experience all of it. To live every moment as something exquisite and entirely new. Maintaining that attitude pre-supposes a sense of inner calm and quiet watchfulness and the abandonment of defensiveness; in short, a sense of wonder. For the instant that barricades and battlements of defensiveness go up, the inspired dream is lost. The price of defensiveness and self protection is the loss of creativity. Fortunately, achievement of inner quietude makes defensiveness unnecessary.

Observing a contemplative internal stillness between efforts to make yourself heard, serves several important purposes. One is the simple conservation of energy, pacing yourself. Second is that you establish a stable, universal center for the spinning thoughts and ideas which appear from nowhere, mutate, solidify and eventually take their place in some creative work. You are able to hear inspiration when it knocks at your door. Too much flapping around and purposeless activity deafens us to the sounds of inspiration's quiet arrival. Third, internal stillness and calm teaches the discipline of "Actively Doing Nothing," a concept I discovered entirely by accident as a result of theater union breaks.

According to union rules, stage crews may work only so many hours without a break. And, when the crew breaks, you are left stranded in the theater with no way to function. You must wait for the workmen to return. To preserve a state of alertness and momentum with nothing to do, I decided to relax and actively do nothing. Sitting quietly, eyes closed, I let everything of the day's activity drift away, then without forcing any particular ideas, noticed what thoughts wandered by. This exercise allows your mind to stroll uninhibited around the block and see what it sees. The thoughts which arose from this process I recorded on a couple note pads and they eventually became the basis for this book. You see, you really have no idea what's on your mind unless you periodically consult your brain. You'll be amazed at what you discover in there lying dormant.

Overall, faith in silence and inner calm, a lack of defensiveness and aggressiveness, bears no real risk. For ultimately, the force of inner calm radiates a sense of purpose, bolstered by the development of your own powerful instincts which, in themselves, provide a strong protection against any random circumstances or individuals not worthy of your trust. And the only route into this inner calm is through dropping the barricades, through floating downstream, through not planning an automatic offensive, through a state of steadfast innocence by means of which your actual peril and vulnerability, paradoxically, are much reduced. For, from the vantage point of a calm, peaceful center it becomes possible to see and intuit very far, to plan for future action instead of a momentary defense.

The best concrete example of this undefended and nonaggressive attitude is that of water. The Taoist philosophy notes that it is impossible to push or bully water, liquid simply moves away. [Likewise, it is impossible to fight with one who will not join the argument.] Water takes its own path; flows peacefully, inexorably, and with the natural force of gravity. And, even without an aggressive agenda, becomes an irresistible force. It makes its way through calm persistence, without turmoil or dissent, flowing over and around obstacles, homeward to the Sea.

Taking on an attitude of floating and flowing preserves strength. And, when you do determine to cease floating and take action, be sure to include two more forces in your arsenal of personal power: honesty and kindness, the everyday versions of truth and love. Oh sure, you say, just try it in this dog-eat-dog world and see how far you get. In fact, working as a troubleshooter I found that attitude is everything. You will almost always encounter what you expect. Walk into a negotiation with a chip on your shoulder and someone will knock it off for you. On the other hand, approach the situation anticipating the best from everyone and that is what you will get. In life, you will find what you expect to find. It is a question of belief. When your intention is honesty and amiability, you will have those in return.

In the field of purchasing, for example, I dealt with some very hard-boiled salesmen who were used to scrapping for the last penny, arm wrestling over every minute detail. I quite simply told them, they knew what was fair and I expected fairness. I would be forthright with them treating them honestly and paying them on time; we would not waste energy grappling for every cent. But, I would expect their most competitive bid and, if they cheated me, they would only do it once. We developed very productive relationships with vendors, better than the company had ever had before. And salesmen bent over backwards with the special purchase arrangements they offered us. We spent all of our effort trying to treat each other right, in an entirely different sort of contest than businessmen most often are used to. We negotiated business in an atmosphere of trust, to our mutual benefit.

In handling insurance settlements, I found the same truths applied. The company had accumulated stacks of files outlining the details of complaints and claims which represented potential court battles. Everyone was arming themselves with lawyers, girding themselves for the fight. On a trial basis, I asked for a fund of money to try to settle some of the arguments myself. The company was more than happy to give it a chance. I invited the complainants to sit down and talk about the incident or damages and how to resolve the problem. Far and away, most people just wanted someone -- a living, breathing human being -- to be sorry. They wanted an apology and to be assured that what was broken would be fixed. Nearly always, the actual cost involved was negligible and the threats and anger on both sides had escalated entirely out of proportion to the individual's injury or the need for the company to defend and refuse reparations without a lawsuit. We averted many unnecessary and expensive legal altercations. It is the same in any arena. Fixing problems and creating a more constructive attitude comes down to our individual expectations of how the world should be, of what is possible. Few people will refuse logic and kindness, the elementary levels of truth and love.

That we will probably get in return what we invest, that our expectations of others will most likely be realized, suggests that, in a sense, we create our own reality. In recent years, that concept is echoed by scientific findings about the nature of the physical world in general. In "The Dancing Wu Li Masters," author Gary Zukav explains in clear layman's terms the mental shift in approach we must make to apprehend the difference between Newtonian physics and the physics represented by quantum mechanics. The obvious difference is that we are no longer measuring evident motion and quantities. In fact, in the subatomic realm of quantum mechanics, we can measure only momentum or position, and only one or the other of those at one time, never both simultaneously. And, in absolute defiance of Newtonian Law, in quantum mechanics, we discover that we are not just observers of an impartial universe and its ruthless,

138

unbiased rules; but are participants in that universe, and quite possibly its creators. This realization has come as a result of experiments which demonstrate that observing the behavior of subatomic particles changes their behavior, may in fact control their behavior. Some physicists are beginning to believe that certain particles come into existence because we wish them to be there, says Gary Zukav.

> Quantum physicists ponder questions like, 'Did a particle with momentum exist before we conducted an experiment to measure its momentum?; 'Did a particle with position exist before we conducted any experiment to measure its position?'; and 'Did any particles exist at all before we thought about them and measured them?' Did we create the particles that we are experimenting with? Incredible as it sounds, this is a possibility that many physicists recognize. John Wheeler, a well-known physicist at Princeton, wrote: May the universe in some strange sense be 'brought into being' by the participation of those who participate? ... The vital act is the act of participation. 'Participator' is the incontrovertible new concept given by quantum mechanics. It strikes down the term 'observer' of classical theory, the man who stands safely behind the thick glass wall and watches what goes on without taking part. It can't be done, quantum mechanics says.

Our universe is not indifferent to our behavior and may actually be the result of our behavior, intentions and emotions. Physics now says that we actively create our own reality. We are not its observers, nor its victims. The substance of which our society, our culture, our universe is composed evolves out of our own aims and desires. Or, in the words of Eastern Indian philosophers: "What appears to be coming at you is actually coming from you." We are in control, the creators who are placing and replacing the building blocks of life every day. We are responsible. No one else.

What extraordinary and wonderful possibilities this presents! If particles can be brought into being through the force or our inner calm and stillness, be made to sing with our honesty and kindness, we will have created the paramount form of beauty and harmony. We will have built a paradise on earth.

We will never get so far by attacking individual social ills and problems, never enact such a far-reaching and all-inclusive solution as this one. In attempting to solve each of the multitude of our cultural problems we address only the symptoms, not the deep rooted deficiencies. For, to paraphrase Shakespeare, our failings lie not in the obvious malignancies of our society, Horatio, but in our selves.

We realize our destiny as human beings, come into our maturity, with the discovery of these miraculous creative abilities, with the understanding that we literally impact physical reality at a subatomic level. With that knowledge, we must prepare to undertake our role as guardians of the universe which has spawned us. No one is exempt in that all of us wield the creative influence of artists, the responsibility to view ourselves as participants, as the shapers of physical existence, the determinants of moral behavior and peace in the galaxy.

This is a feminine, an intuitive, a nurturing process, the essential missing ingredient in all of history. And in this era we finally must bring the inventiveness and strength of masculinity and the sensitivity and caring of femininity to a balance. We have exercised our muscles long enough, marveling at our abilities to construct and administer; and now, with tenderness and compassion, should breathe the beauty of which we are capable into all creation.

Of course, finding valid examples of such a way of life becomes increasingly difficult. A glance at the newspaper headlines and anyone can testify that nearly every country on the globe is rent by war, poverty, racism, disease, hatred and despair of every variety. I am sure there are those who will say, "Beauty? Harmony? Look, we have real problems, why talk about beauty at a time like this?" Because what we are able to visualize of paradise will be the way out of our misery. And since we will attain what we expect, let's fix our gaze on the ultimate.

I realize that much of the world probably forgets what Beauty looks like. For instance, there's not much left of the Mediterranean wonderland of Beirut. Large parts of South Africa, Ireland, Czechoslovakia, Cambodia, Somalia, Afghanistan, Iraq, Guatemala, Libya, Columbia, Kuwait, Grenada, Israel, Yugoslavia, Pakistan, El Salvador and Iran, have been bombed off the map. A once lovely Geneva, Switzerland now bears a reputation as "Needle City," and as a growing center of crime and crack cocaine consumption. Many cities, in fact, are unfit for habitation by the law-abiding among us. The day belongs to artists like Isaac Stern and Zubin Mehta who performed in Jerusalem under missile fire from Iraq; who in the midst of imminent danger were only strengthened in their determination to bring beauty to the people of that beleaguered city, to an audience who listened in eerie silence, wearing gas masks.

If that is where we have come, we cannot afford to relinquish the torch now. There is no one way to accomplish anything, no one technique or method. Yet, great importance resides in the encouragement of example; the example that the achievement of a dream lies within the grasp of all of us. And the artist tells us, "Despite everything, you too may stand here, you may achieve near perfection. Beauty is possible."

Establishing a new goal takes only the first several of us to set the mark. After all, for hundreds of years there were hundreds of reasons why no man alive could run a mile in under four minutes. Then Roger Bannister did it. And six weeks later, someone beat his record. Now over eight hundred people have done the same. We should learn from the pacesetters.

I assure you beauty and harmony are not just achievable but are our destiny. The only question is how we will come to them. And, if by some sad misfortune you can find no examples of these lovely abstracts on which to attach your vision, your goal, please visit backstage at the nearest opera company, where you may hear and feel the heart of Beauty, the pulse of Harmony, beating steadily.

Chapter Eleven

Nothing draws music-lovers to the opera like the romantic, playful and poignant masterpiece, "La Boheme." Extra performances had been added to accommodate as many Puccini fans as possible. And, in the midst of the excited and happy crowd I found myself, once again, a ticket holder, a civilian theater-goer.

Even so, from the moment the curtain rose, it was obvious that my experience of attending opera was changed forever. The staging, cues, and lighting effects stood out as though in bas-relief. I would never again view an operatic performance as seamless and completely mysterious. Now I would be watching for all the nuance, searching for inventive and innovative staging concepts and, above all, keeping my fingers crossed for the performers and crew. I could imagine cues being called through the head sets from backstage to the orchestra pit, dressing rooms and lighting booth. I consciously watched effects fade in and out. It was an entirely different view; and fortunately one I happened to enjoy. Jonathon Field had a distinctive, light, contemporary style of direction. I wished I had been able to work with him.

On our ride from the airport, tenor Joseph Wolverton had confided that his last trip to Arizona proved nothing short of disastrous. During his engagement as Pinkerton in "Madame Butterfly" he contracted an infection of the vocal chords which, although not painful, left him mystified about the sudden unpredictability of his voice. He never forgot the frightening experience. He hoped the audience had. If the standing ovation he received for his portrayal of Rodolfo was any indication of the sentiment, his worries are over. Knowing Wolverton's trepidation and witnessing his triumph lent an additional layer of meaning to this performance, and yet another reason to especially enjoy the evening. It is always fun to see someone win.

Unlike everything I had undertaken in the past in a multitude of varied career opportunities, opera was a truly bottomless challenge, and an endless delight. The mere complexity of the art form, wide variations in musical style, language, and historic background; the artistry of costuming and make-up, requirements of lighting and special effects, to say nothing of the personal element and inherent difficulties of live performance, imbue opera production with an eternal sense of a new creation. Even from one performance to the next, opera is never the same twice. With the same cast, crew, orchestra, director, conductor, theater, every performance stands out as its own event, its own creative effort. I often wonder how critics could not know this, and that they actually believe they can predict for an audience what the next performance will be like based upon their single evening in the theater. That certainty is literally impossible -- as the experience of the next production, "The Marriage of Figaro," proved to me with resounding authority.

The day after we saw "La Boheme," I convened a conference with my children. Would they mind, I asked them, if I signed on with the production team for "Figaro?" They would have to be as invested in the idea as I to make it work out for everyone since, once more, life would have to revolve around rehearsal schedule. They had three questions: Would they be invited, as before, to sit in on rehearsal? Would they get to talk with conductor Henry Holt again? Would I introduce them to the singers? With affirmative answers on all counts, they threw in their lots.

When I contacted Nina, she simply said, "We start music on Sunday. Plan to be here and we'll see where you fit in."

Her hesitation in not assigning me to a definite position was based, I found out, on the professional style of the stage director. James Lucas' style is that of a veteran, a consummate expert, a one-man band, a professor of stage direction at Indiana University who has directed opera in every major house from the Metropolitan to San Francisco. He knows exactly what he is looking for from each performer, every note in the score, every syllable of the libretto. There is simply not one shred of impromptu interpretation or guesswork. He does not suffer fools gladly.

Said Nina, "Jim doesn't use assistants. He sees no need for them. He works from a format that turns out beautiful traditional operatic productions, on time, and always well within budget. From an administrative point of view, he is a gem. He is also a perfectionist and I have seen him reduce seasoned stage managers to tears."

In other words, this man would prefer not to deal with amateurs, with bumbling beginners, however well-intentioned. Still, Nina suggested I stick around and see what might happen. Sitting in on the music-only rehearsals gave me confidence things might work out. Henry Holt had returned as guest conductor. Coming into the hall, he ignored the handshake I offered and hugged me.

"Welcome back," he said. "Handshakes are no longer appropriate. We've been through too much together for that."

After a preliminary musical run-through with the principal singers, he added, "I think you'll stay with us and we'll finally see you up there on the stage."

Doing what, I couldn't imagine. Just so long as I wasn't mopping the stage floor after the performance, I thought.

The day staging rehearsals began, Nina introduced me to Jim Lucas, and I carefully kept my distance to observe him in action, sitting behind the piano with Music Director, Dean Ryan, who accompanied the rehearsals, following his score.

Jim Lucas was indeed informed, definite, and absolutely professional. At the end of rehearsal, Nina asked me to drive him home. However, once out the door, he suggested something different.

"Take me someplace for dinner," he said, "I haven't had a thing to eat all day."

As we drove, I tried to explain why I wanted to work with him.

"I realize," I said, "My presence here probably isn't your idea of a dream come true. But I want to learn a lot more than I know. And it seems to me the best way to learn is from experience."

At the restaurant, we spent two hours talking about favorite performers, composers, conductors and theaters; about critics, stage direction, opera on film, and everything else under the operatic sun. And Jim Lucas told me several of the multitude of fascinating recollections from his many years in the performing arts.

As we left the restaurant, heading for the car, Mr. Lucas stopped walking, turned, and said, "If you want to be in this business, I'm your man. Stick by me in rehearsal. Stop me anytime. Ask me anything you want. I'll teach you all I can."

Who could ask for more than that? Over the next three weeks, I enjoyed a wonderful association with a kind and generous mentor.

The experience of producing "The Marriage of Figaro" could not have been more different than that of "The Valkyrie" if it had been an entirely different art form. Where Wagner is epic, tragic and convoluted; Mozart was ingenuous, comic, and elegant. Mozart's artlessness, however, should not be construed to be simplistic. His is a style of ingenious complexity, living right on the surface of a seemingly simple melody.

Or, as Music Director Dean Ryan phrased his comparison of Mozart with Italian opera, "The challenge of Mozart is that there are no garlic bushes to hide behind."

Mozart's apparently straightforward melodies must be interpreted, not only with precision, but also with musicality, intelligence and a light touch, or in place of art you will have only artifice.

The Arizona Opera Company is the only company in the United States which consistently plays a full operatic season in two cities, Tucson and Phoenix, besides adding a third dimension of performances in the Wagner Festival. Yet, even for so accomplished a Company, production of Mozartian opera constitutes a special challenge, because of the huge, hollow dimensions of the both theatres in which the opera plays, described in the industry as "barns." These facilities, the Tucson Music Hall and the Phoenix Symphony Hall are big general-use houses exceeding twenty five hundred seats with no accoustical preparation whatsoever in accomodation of opera.

The set which was leased for the "Figaro" production attested to the normally smaller stage size. Mr. Ross added a portal, a large decorative frame, at the grand curtain to blend and off-set a rake decidedly smaller than the one we had used for "Die Walküre." Several singers thought this produced extra resonance. Still, they faced a substantial challenge in projecting predominantly light and airy melodies over such a cavernous expanse. However, in some compensation, the frantically comic aspect of "Figaro" offers great potential for inventive stage direction during scenes in which characters are secreted away in closets, hidden behind furniture and bushes, disguised in dresses and cloaks, stashed away in gazebos.

"The Marriage of Figaro" constitutes a musical version of the French play of the same title by Pierre-Augustin Caron de Beaumarchais; a comedy which poked all manner of fun at aristocracy, and served as yet another nail in the coffin of royalty immediately prior to the outbreak of the French revolution. Mozart was able to stage his opera in Vienna only through the intercession of famed librettist, Lorenzo da Ponte, who convinced the Emperor that all the political sting had been removed in the translation from play to opera. Despite assertions that he had diluted the bite of criticism in his interpretation of Beaumarchais' "Figaro," Mozart managed to leave firmly intact the resounding censure of the amount of power which often is placed in the hands of immoral and undeserving men simply because of their monied, influential heritage. Who says classic opera is not contemporary?

The complex storyline of "Figaro" is based upon the complications which develop because the n'er-do-well Count Almaviva rescinded the "droit du seigneur" in his castle upon his marriage to the beautiful Rossina. In doing so, Almaviva gave up his right to the wedding night with any woman of his domain who married. This he has done in deference to his servants -- that is until Figaro proposes to Susanna, Countess Almaviva's lovely chambermaid. Count Almaviva's attempts to maneuver and reclaim his right with Susanna, his deceptions of his wife and of Figaro, versus the plotting of all three in defiance of the Count, make this a musically rich, comic and exciting opera.

Subplots which point out the corruption of lawyers and of the legal system of the day (sound familiar?), as well as the presence of an overheated adolescent, Cherubino, who vies with the Count for the attentions of the ladies, add additional dimensions of comedy and political satire.

As current as much of this is, it certainly represented even headier stuff, transmitted many additional overtones, in the eighteenth century. For example, Jim Lucas took special pains to gain sympathy for the poor Countess in her luckless position. Newly married with a faithless cad for a husband and no chance of a divorce, she was trapped.

In fact, at one rehearsal, Lucas turned from the stage and said to me specifically, but to cast and crew in general, "Of course the Countess realizes at the end, even though the Count has begged her forgiveness, she will go through all of this many more times. And you have to understand the basis for her forgiving him. This poor lady has no alternative. She must defer to the Count. Her only option is a nunnery, which Lucas explained really can't be considered a choice for a lady of social standing and style.

"Oh really," I said, "How's the food?"

It's not funny though, the advantage that is taken of power and position. And even less funny that more than two hundred years after this opera was composed, we still place people in positions of leadership for all the wrong reasons. Working on "Figaro," I thought about why this still occurs and came to the conclusion that we place weak people at the head of government because we think they will do as we want. And yet we probably have no better chance of that happening than the Countess did of keeping track of her wandering husband.

We are confusing statesmanship with salesmanship when we believe a leader will and can respond to our personal agenda. Too many separate, conflicting interests exist for any president, governor or congressman to appeal to a significant proportion of them simultaneously. Those who believe they elected a leader to act as their pawn will, by the law of averages, be sadly mistaken. And, I resent the fact that officials who owe their position to mercenary financial support and purchased votes spend their time in office greasing palms and repaying favors instead of representing the people.

Government should be composed of those who are most morally and spiritually fit to lead, not of those placed in power as the result of some popular platform, political party or political agenda. Any reasonably intelligent person can hear the facts and make sensible decisions in government. And leaders would be better off without a lot of preconceived, canned and dictated notions of what to do. An open mind is indispensable in most situations. Yet, the politically motivated rule our lives. That amounts to little more than survival of the fittest, the rule of the wolf pack.

We need instead the public servant who is morally and spiritually fit for the job, who makes decisions based upon an unerring sense of values, not based upon political favors owed. Leaders should be elected in recognition of their character, not their promises. Most emphatically, officials, elected or appointed, should not just do whatever we command. They should do what is right. Common sense says that if all of us individually with our diverse interests could wrestle this country between us, push and pull it down a proper path, we could dispense with government entirely. We know that is not possible.

Yet, the current system invites dissent of all kinds. At the very least, anyone who did not elect a particular leader reserves the right to a continuing protest throughout that official's tenure in office. What a waste of energy. Whether you voted for a particular leader or not, the majority did. And, in a democracy, the new incoming government should be given a chance to prove itself without the distractions of second-guessing from among the ranks. More than anything else, we need unity. We hobble our leaders with our uninformed, prejudiced and warring demands. To be united behind a decision, even if it is flawed, is preferable to constant dissent. Common concern will illuminate the nature of the flaw and correct it. The original concept of a balance of powers did not include an inflammatory media and a kibbitzing, self-interested public. It included three branches of government united in protection of a sacred trust.

I saw the power of unity at work during the production of "Figaro" in a situation which could only be described as having the potential for all out disaster. The Tucson run of performances had been flawless. After opening night, every performance in both cities was sold out immediately. On the day we were to open in Phoenix to a Standing Room Only crowd, with just six hours before the curtain, our leading lady became extremely ill. Mr. Ross began a rapid search for a replacement. His only other choice would be to cancel Phoenix's opening night. He decided to fly Laurel Boyd in from California, a singer who had sung Susanna in concert, but never in a fully staged production. Landing in Phoenix at four o'clock for a seven thirty curtain, this poor woman did not even have time for a full run through with the other performers. All the vocalists rallied to help her.

Meanwhile, the rest of us, as we boarded the buses in Tucson, headed for work at the Phoenix theatre, heard the news and understood Mr. Ross's decision to go ahead with the performance. Stage manager David Boone and I were more or less on our own by this point. Director Jim Lucas had flown out for an engagement in New York City the day before we opened in Tucson. So, we put our heads together to isolate all Susanna's cues in the score and to highlight any scene which required her to carry on props. He suggested he and I split stage left and stage right responsibilities for keeping track of Susanna and cueing her specifically. It seemed, if Laurel Boyd's nerves didn't shatter, we could manage.

Two traffic jams later, we and the chorus were late in arriving at the theater. There would be no time for supper, which upset the chorus, but suited me just fine, my stomach was in a knot anyway.

We did a quick check on the scenery, props and electrical setup. If you've never explored the backstage area of a theater, you should go have a look. It's a fascinating world of its own. What the audience actually sees from the theater equates with looking in the picture window of a four story house. They never realize there's a basement, a second floor, and an attic with all sorts of activity going on in them. Behind the curtain, the stage soars several stories upward. Here scenery and curtains are suspended by counterweights and connected lines are tied off at the "pin rail," from which everything is hauled up and down by a system of pullies. Anything that drops from the ceiling is said to "fly." The main curtain is referred to as the "grand." Fixed curtains which screen all of the sideline activity of the crew from view are referred to as "masking," and provide exit and entrance areas for performers. Most communication takes place on an open channel via headsets, consisting of an earpiece and microphone. This connects performance managers on both sides of the stage with the dressing rooms, wardrobe area, the electricians, sound technician, props master, surtitle projectionist, spot light operators and lighting technicians.

During intermissions, scenery may be rolled or dollied around or flown in and out from the ceiling, making set changes something of an exotic, technical ballet. Dressing rooms, wardrobe areas, practice rooms, and so forth are often housed conveniently off the wings -- or inconveniently downstairs beneath the stage. And the orchestra pit entrance will usually be underneath the stage as well. All performers and crew are kept in contact with the performance in progress through sound monitors which broadcast the live performance and carry announcements from the stage manager.

Downstairs at the Phoenix orchestra pit, Henry Holt shook his head. Two productions before, the pit area had been drastically reconfigured to accommodate the larger orchestra of "The Valkyrie" in tiers. These changes were left intact for the remaining productions of the Wagnerian Ring Cycle. Seating all the players of the much smaller "Figaro" orchestra on the first tier meant that the string section was so cramped Henry could not squeeze into the pit from stage right where my communications headset was wired at the top of the stairs above a gigantic two-story rehearsal hall, from which I was to cue his entrance. He would have to enter from the staircase opposite and I would need to cue him in pantomime from approximately thirty yards away, without being noticed by the waiting audience.

"Semaphore might be good," Henry suggested. We would wing it, we agreed. Which turned out to be a good deal more difficult than anticipated.

Testing headset communications, we found a mysterious open line. Everything from stage left was broadcasting over the house through a speaker no one seemed able to locate. Repeated efforts to fix this failed. Nina's voice could be heard everywhere.

"Maybe I should sing," she offered wryly.

Miraculously, pushing several buttons on the stage manager's console, David Boone finally shut the feedback off just as the audience entered.

We had discovered on running some time tests of the grand curtain that the lining billowed and caught on the extra portal that had been added to balance the scenery. The curtain had to be rung down slowly, in stages, taking twelve seconds (a literal eternity), an interesting effect at best.

"I hate electric and hydraulic equipment," the operator of the grand curtain told me.

He had worked on several stages with hydraulic equipment, he said, and had never liked the fact that, with automatic pullies, you couldn't feel what was happen. Even if everything was snagged, the motor kept right on moving until something snapped.

"All you see," he said, "is digital numbers flying on the monitor. You have no sense of tension on the lines, you don't have any idea what's going on.

"Why one time," he said, "Without knowing it, we got a stage manager tangled in the rigging and she hung up there for four hours until we could get her down." He winked at me.

I laughed, knowing I was the new kid on the block and, in the vast extended family of the opera company, I was fair game. The company already had an established joke about one of my stage management responsibilities in "Figaro." David Boone had asked me to take care of the repetitive sound effects which simulate doors being locked and unlocked during the Act Two hysteria in the Countess's bedroom. In this scene, the furious

Count closes and locks every door he can, trying to corner and capture the would-be lover Cherubino.

Soon, everyone from the principles, to the chorus, stage crew and wardrobe personnel were teasing about my "world debut as the doorlock in Act Two." Even the young Vietnamese seamstress who knew little English and never said two words to anybody came backstage to joke about my "wonderful performance."

Said Henry, "I can't believe it. The critics never mentioned our doorlock in the reviews." I laughed as hard as anybody and enjoyed it all. It was their way of recognizing and including me.

At quarter past seven, Mr. Ross walked the stage with Laurel Boyd as she viewed the set and met all of us for the first time. Then, he stepped before the audience and explained the conditions under which we would proceed. They seemed appreciative that he had made a substitution and kept the performance schedule. Across the downstairs chasm, with a series of enthusiastic calisthenics, I signaled Henry Holt into the pit and the overture began.

Laurel Boyd was a marvel. She may have been on the verge of a nervous breakdown, but she seemed in complete control, even chatting between entrances. Certainly, the bass who played Figaro, Herbert Perry, was a seasoned performer and provided tremendous support. Still, I could not believe Laurel's calm and command of the situation. She played a very lively and vivacious Susanna. So lively, in fact, that during the Second Act, the buttons on the back of her dress gradually undid themselves. On her next entrance, Korby Myrick, our Cherubino, sang from behind Susanna and methodically rebuttoned her costume.

Except for the ongoing problems with the grand curtain, everything went flawlessly until the end of the Act Three. The program called for a two minute pause for a quick scenery change during which we would drop a small "show curtain" in front of the rake. This served as a backdrop for Barbarina's aria at the beginning of Act Four, after which the show curtain is raised to reveal the garden and gazebo of the finale.

And, in this situation, disaster threatened once more. The show curtain was snarled in the rigging overhead and would not shake loose. The planned two minute lag turned into four minutes.

The stage manager asked me to go down to the pit and alert the conductor to the problem. I ran downstairs, but soon remembered the stage right side of the orchestra pit was packed solid with string players. Henry could not see me. Besides, his gaze was firmly focused on the stage, waiting patiently for the show curtain to drop. I could hardly march out there in plain view of the audience. So, in desperation, I crawled into the orchestra on my hands and knees and had made my way through the violins into the cello section, by the time Henry noticed me. To his credit, he stepped from the podium as though we were following some time-honored procedure and knelt beside me on the floor, to the astonishment of the musicians. Our exchange complete, I slithered back out.

In a few moments, one of the crew climbed up into the rigging and released the tangled chains of the show curtain and things went forward, just a little behind schedule. The show ultimately closed to a wildly enthusiastic standing ovation from the audience, especially for Laurel Boyd, a truly spectacular performer. And, it later occurred to me that the audience knew nothing, really, of all our crises and problems. Even with the substitution of a principle singer, traffic jams, tangled curtains, sound problems, and cramped quarters in the orchestra, the audience was essentially unaware of the hair-raising evening our crew had spent. And that is what professionalism is about. You just make it work.

It is as Gio Ross, head of wardrobe, tells everyone who tries to make off-handed recommendations about costuming: the important feature is for everyone to stick to their own job, their own concerns, make their piece of the production click. In rehearsal, the stage director rules and, on stage, the stage manager prevails.

"We placed these people in charge," she says, "Let them do their job."

154

That is how the company takes direction.   No second-guessing, no duplication of leadership or effort.   Within this closely knit organization, each person must know their own role and carry out their responsibilities to the letter.   Otherwise, chaos reigns.   Everyone stands in support of the leader and follows the same direction.   Regardless of personal differences and agendas, regardless of quirks and foibles, everyone gives to the performance, to the overall effort, to making it work.   I wish we could get that straight in relation to leadership throughout the world in general.

The prize for forbearance following "The Operatic Night in Hell," goes to an exhausted chorus singer who sat behind me on the bus between two other vocalists for the return trip home.   It sounded as though he was running a one a.m. emergency session of the United Nations.

"Look, I'm really tired," he said.   "And I don't mind speaking with you in Italian, and it's alright if Vladimir talks to me in Russian.   But, please, not both at once."   Only on an opera bus.

The day Jim Lucas had left for New York I told him I hoped to work with him again some day.

"I'm directing here in September," he said, "Start working on the "Die Fledermaus" score and I'll see you then.

The night "Figaro" closed, Nina seconded his idea.

"You have certainly paid your dues," she said. "I know that sounds trite and if I had a hundred more ways to say it I would. Do you want a job? I mean a paying job."

I didn't even ask what it was. I accepted.

A week after the opera season concluded, another hurdle vanished.   The financial settlement of our personal estate was finalized.   I let out a sigh of relief.   At last, the children and I would begin to have our own funds to spend as we pleased.

"What will you do, Mama?" Rachel asked.   "What are your priorities? Have you thought about it?"

Oh yes. I had thought all that through in detail and the plan was clear.

"First," I said, "We spend a day at 'Gadabout Spa.' Then, we stop at the lingerie sale at 'Victoria's Secret.' I need some new piano music and a compact disc recording of 'Die Fledermaus.' Oh yes, and perfume. And that should put me in a frame of mind to figure out the rest of our rosie future."

Rachel laughed. "You know, Mama, poverty hasn't changed you a bit. You're still an overgrown child and a shameless hedonist."

Ah yes, a difficult, dangerous job, but someone had to do it.

Chapter Twelve

We laughed about the love of luxury, of creature comforts, which lingered as a superficial remnant of the past, but Rachel and I both knew that nothing was essentially the same. The tectonic plates underground had shifted irreversibly and surface reverberations would undoubtedly continue for some time. Yet, several new and more predictable forces had arisen which more than compensated for the quaking and chaos. Writing and opera imparted a new sense of focus to the world; established for the first time a magnetic North and a gravitational pull. Out of the formlessness were born spiritual stars to steer by and the latitude and longitude of practical goals. Even adrift on the Sea, I had a center and the means to plot a course.

In fact, in one short year from the time of the plunge to the Sea, every single facet of life had been replaced. And if, in the beginning, someone had given me a conscious choice, had said, "Take this risk, and in one year, you will have traded your career, marriage, luxurious home, longstanding friendships, bank account and secure lifestyle for a yet-to-be-named job at the Arizona opera, a half-finished book, financial uncertainty, and an apartment, I would have thought the recommendation insane. Yet, I had made that trade, based on a nameless faith and faceless inspiration. And, amazingly, had yet to regret anything about it.

Of my many fears, the largest was that of being selfish; that changing life "to suit myself" would alienate the children and spoil their childhood. That turned out to be an unfounded worry. The children have benefited notably. At a simplistic level, they are happier because I am happier. But beyond that, each of their lives has expanded in ways no one could have predicted. I now know that children learn far more from example than from instructions, lessons and lectures. When I established an office at home to begin writing, Rachel set up her own art studio in the next room to work close by. We since have come to agree that inspiration begets inspiration; something I had already experienced at the opera. The influence of the singers' creative process set my mind wheeling from one thought to the next in rapid succession. At rehearsal breaks, the residual energy in the theater left me scribbling furiously, sketching out the schematics, skeletal bones and shadows, of seemingly endless and intriguing revelations.

Working side-by-side at home, Rachel and I found the same to be true. As "the Book" evolved, she filled the walls with a gallery of anthropomorphic self-portraits in charcoal, pencil, and oil colors, which brought her features and personality to life in rainbow shades and in black and white: the reclining figure of a majestic lion. Previously fearful of leaving home for college, she initiated applications with several art schools in Lacoste and Aix-en-Provence, France. And, after five years of half-hearted effort, she became a serious student of the clarinet.

The process of transformation remolded the younger children as well. Remarkably, when we began paring down our furnishings to the dimensions of an apartment, the first item eliminated --by their choice -- was the gigantic television. They didn't need it, they said, they were just too busy with other pursuits: writing and illustrating books, building instruments from old tools and containers to create their own "garage" concert band, even trying their hand at composing an opera. Both auditioned for the Arizona Children's Choir and were accepted. Daniel took up the violin; Adrienne the cello.

And they retained all their usual ties with friends, their love of sports and games, books and toys, the standard pre-occupations of childhood. Over time, I watched their confidence and self-concept grow and improve as they strove to find and follow my tracks into this new life. Certainly, this cannot have been an easy year for them, facing the pain and realities of divorce. And yet, being able to express themselves in every possible way, dispensing with the automated entertainment of television in favor of putting their own creations onto paper, canvas; pouring out their emotion into the strings of an instrument or a chorus of song, would seem to have preserved them from permanent harm. The depth of their metamorphosis, that it vastly exceeded anything attributable to innocent mimicry, became apparent later on when Daniel unveiled the subject of his first operatic libretto. I shouldn't have been so taken by surprise. I had read about it all before in Joseph Campbell's book, "Myths to Live By."

It was Joseph Campbell's contention that every culture and religion known to man have shared identical mythologies to which we all subconsciously subscribe, by means of which we are all subliminally connected. Every religion tells a story of creation similar in many ways to that of the Bible. All cultures recount some version of the search for the Grail, of Oedipus the King and the epic Hero Journey. These mythologies have seemed to arise, not so much out of fantasy and storytelling, as out of the primal nature of human beings, out of an innate knowing and believing. Campbell explained that we use these mythologies, whether consciously or unconsciously, comparing our experiences with those of legend, building a metaphorical and symbolic structure to interpret milestone events in our lives. He ultimately coordinated several lectures with psychiatrist, Dr. John Weir Perry, who added another dimension to the theory: that an inability to assimilate this intercultural mythology equates with insanity, especially with schizophrenia.

Several years ago, in the midst of researching information about the North American Plains Indian rite of the vision quest (in which the tribal elders send adolescents through a ritual journey into the wilderness to seek a vision and find maturity), I had contacted John Perry to ask about the comparison of his philosophy with that of a typical rite of passage. He graciously agreed to explain his views in more detail.

Perry believes that most often people have the capability to delve into their own psyche and keep themselves emotionally fit. In fact, a veritable handful cannot adjust their own psyche and become insane. Usually, we work out our personal mythology in dreams and fantasies, he said. And, across the world, across cultures, seem to recognize and indulge in a remarkably similar symbolism and mythological frame of reference.

In particular, Perry was adamant that even severely schizophrenic patients should not be drugged and tortured with shock treatments. Instead, he said, they should be treated by apt physicians who can follow their delusion and identify the place at which the patient has become derailed from their internal mythology. Mental health, according to Perry, relies upon the subconscious experience of living out macrocosmic dreams and, failing that, falters and becomes twisted into the torment of the relentless waking nightmare of schizophrenia.

Unlike traditional psychiatrists, Perry preferred to get down into the terrifying snake-pit of insanity with the patient and live out their terror with them, helping them tell and reconstruct their personal mythology. An exhausting and heartbreaking occupation, however, often a fulfilling undertaking, Perry said, particularly in early cases with young adults where he found miraculous successes.

With my research complete, I filed away the interview with Dr. Perry and thought little about it again. Until one evening at rehearsal in the Tucson Music Hall when, in a conversation with Maestro Henry Holt and his wife, operatic soprano Rebecca Ravenshaw, Daniel unveiled the plot of an opera he intended to compose. All of my children were fascinated with the epic story of "Die Walküre," particularly admiring the stature of characters of heroic and god-like proportions like Wotan and Brunnhilde.

"I'm writing the sequel to 'Die Walküre,'" Daniel told Henry and Rebecca.

I was sitting in front of them, working with stage director, Claus Koenig, and turned around to make a flippant comment that the sequel, in fact several of them, had been written. My children love talking with Henry because he listens with such respect to their ideas. The seriousness of Henry's face as he considered what Daniel said stopped my joking in midair. I listened too.

"What is the title of your opera?" Henry asked.

"The Troll King," Daniel said.

Henry asked to hear the story and Daniel immediately obliged. The plot revolved around five characters: the King, the Queen, the Prince, the Troll, and the Angel. In Act I, Scene One, the King, Queen and Prince live happily in the palace. By Scene Two, dark clouds blow over and everything turns for the worse. The King, said Daniel, goes into the evil forest and comes home each day in a foul frame of mind. He has little to say to the Queen and Prince who miss him and are very sad. As the King chooses to stay away for longer and longer periods of time, he becomes as evil as the evil forest. Eventually, an Angel attempts to rectify the situation by appearing to the King and warning him to change his ways.

She tells the King that terrible consequences will befall him otherwise. The King just laughs. The next day, he sets out into the forest, going deeper into the undergrowth than ever before, in defiance of the Angel. Suddenly, he is completely encompassed by a dense thicket of thorns, which grow rapidly skyward, making his escape impossible.

The Prince, hearing his father's screams of terror, attempts to cut through the thorns with his sword. He chops for hours, ultimately penetrating to the center of the thicket, where he finds a hideous Troll. The Prince takes a single horrified look and drives the sword through The Troll's heart, then searches frantically for his father. As the Troll dies, the King's features become visible on the awful creature's face and the Prince realizes what he has done. He has slain his own father. He is in agony. The Angel appears. She absolves the Prince and tells him he had to kill the Troll to protect the Queen. She sends the Prince home to his mother. The Queen, said Daniel, mourns the death of the King, but eventually marries a different King and everyone lives happily from that time on.

Daniel concluded his story with enthusiastic innocence, leaving three adults with tears in their eyes. By the conclusion we had all realized, this eight year old child was unwittingly recounting his own mythology of his parents' divorce.

"Where did the idea for your story come from?" Henry asked.

"I dreamed it," Daniel said.

I had gone to great lengths to try to impress upon the children that nothing of the situation was their fault. I had divorced, not they. We talked for hours about how life would go forward, ways in which we would try to keep everything as normal as possible. But the reality of how Daniel interpreted these events had just been painted before my eyes.

"What will I do?" I asked Henry. "I can't let him go on feeling this terrible responsibility."

"Talk to him," he said, "He is a very bright little boy. Very perceptive."

On the way home, I casually asked Daniel to explain the story again. He recounted nearly word for word the version he had told at the theater. And then, I thought of Dr. Perry. Would it help if we rewrote the story together, I wondered?

"Well," I said, "It must have been a very sad dream." Daniel acknowledged it was.

"It will make a very sad opera," I said. "Is that the kind of music you had hoped to write? I thought you liked Mozart. His music is usually happier than that."

Daniel thought. Yes, he would rather write happy music, he admitted. The movie "Amadeus" is his favorite, mostly because of the music.

"I know," he said, "Let's change the story to a happier one."

And, from the beginning, we rewrote Daniel's tragic epic. I asked a lot of questions. What if the forest were not evil, just a different place the King happened to like better than the palace? What if the Queen was just as pleased that the King moved away? What if the Angel appeared to offer help to the Queen rather than to threaten? What if the Queen and King were happier with the whole arrangement? By the time we had finished, the King and Queen parted amiably, and for the best. The Prince became a scientific inventor and wrote operas in his spare time. He was loved by both parents, welcome in the green forest and in the sunny palace.

"I like it better," said Daniel. "I'm going to write the opera and Henry Holt will conduct it. And, maybe I'll even sing the part of the Prince.

Somehow, I'm sure he will.

Regardless of the common underlying themes of the "monomyth" which Campbell proposed all of us innately share, I feel certain Daniel would not have come upon his vividly symbolic dream so readily without the influence of the opera "Die Walküre," an epic drama he had watched with rapt attention throughout a month of rehearsals. The art of his own culture lead him to his subconscious symbolism. Which supported my own belief that what we regard as complex theater, too difficult and tedious for children, is actually a source of concrete inspiration to them which exceeds anyone's wildest expectations. Opera is poetry with an orchestral accompaniment. A more potent elixir does not exist.

Children can readily understand and enjoy opera from about age five. At least, that's when everyone at our house joins the competition for the spare ticket. The rules for attendance are simple. First, you must learn the story of the performance and be able to explain it. Second, you must behave or you will be taken home. This approach succeeded with all three children. They understand and enjoy the show, more so perhaps than many adults. And, realizing immediately that they are the only children in the theater, they know why good behavior is indispensable.

The administration of the Arizona Opera recognizes the powerful connection between children and musical theater. Each production schedule allows for a Children's Dress Rehearsal which admits approximately two thousand elementary school students for what is presumably their first experience in opera. These children are enthralled by what they see. I've attended three of these performances and been amazed that every child pays attention and applauds the performance enthusiastically.

The same is true of children who visit our home and are virtually unfamiliar with classical music. I have never met a child who didn't enjoy an operatic movie, a recording of an instrumental or vocal concert, once they understood what they were hearing. We assume this to be beyond children's comprehension and that is a shame.

Meanwhile, several people who know I am writing a book about the value of music and of artistic inspiration have suggested a chapter panning "that horrible rock music."

"Why?," I asked.

"Because," they tell me, "It's all about sex and violence."

So is a lot of opera and other classic art.

As Claus Koenig said to me at the Children's Performance of "Die Walküre," -- "Do you realize, we just invited two thousand fifth grade children to watch a show about incest and murder?"

And yet, we know that is not what the opera is "about" at all. Any Art is "about" the emotions and values it inspires. With continued discussion, you will find that what really concerns these parents is that rock music has been used by children to fill a spiritual void, a gaping hole in the fabric of life. In many homes, the only exposure children have to the Arts is presented to them through television, movies, and popular songs: primarily disposable art. Life is a sitcom with a laugh track, or a series of canned, airbrushed emotions packaged into an hour and a half of video tape, or a movie soundtrack. Not at all what Daniel saw live on stage when a commanding baritone named Edward Crafts put on a winged helmet and flowing metallic robes, and for four magical hours became a god. A god of mysticism, of love, of anger, of revenge, and ultimately of agony. No flimsily constructed popular music, no sitcom, will ever measure up to that in Daniel's eyes; any more than newspaper cartoons could substitute for the pages of "War and Peace."

Nor should we "sandbag" all of popular culture. Certainly artists create new art every day which deserves serious consideration. But that, I think, is not what worries parents. They share the concerns that author Allan Bloom expressed in "The Closing of the American Mind," that while music is omnipresent in our lives and holds the greatest cultural and emotional sway with youth, the themes expounded upon too often glorify drugs, violence, hatred, and promiscuous behavior. And when any art form is misused we would be better off without it.

On the other hand, what leaves children open to the influence of such music? Aesthetic education begins very early and is first the responsibility of parents. Early education to beauty and enlightenment sets the tone for everything else a child may learn and enjoy in life and should not be misunderstood as optional as "the icing on the cake." Art teaches spiritual values, promotes the expression of the elemental material of the soul. The creation of noble people requires participation in the nobler forms of Art. The mediocrity of popular Art, and lack of parental influence to appreciate anything else, says Bloom, prepares young people for nothing but additional mediocrity.

And, it is his concern, not so much that the vast majority ultimately will aspire to drugs, violence and promiscuity, but that their ability to be truly educated is destroyed, that all enthusiasm and philosophic sensibility has been drained from their lives, that the connection between their human and animal nature will never be clear to them. And, as a result, these young people will aspire only to the lowest levels of learning and spirituality.

Artistic snobbishness, manifested as feeding the generality of mankind popular pablum in place of noble Art, came into fashion some time ago. Only the wealthy and cultured could understand Art, some proposed. In "Music of the Spheres," author Jamie James explains the decline of classical music from the popular scene as the emergence of "musical snobbery." Composer Hector Berlioz devoted much of his critical writings to the contention that "music is not for everyone, nor everyone for music." What nonsense. The uneducated were to be shut out and forever forbidden the ability to become educated. Perhaps a lack of universal literacy at the time prevented more of an outcry against such a pathetic cultural ruling. But, maybe it is not too late to take back our children's birthright.

Fine music must be for everyone. We are composed ninety percent of water and none of us would dream of going without it. We are composed one hundred percent of music; how long can human beings live and thrive without the restoration of their own essence? And when we take a drink, we look for aqua pura, not mud. Mediocrity begets mediocrity. Inspiration begets inspiration. It is that simple.

We cannot damn any form of music based solely upon a key signature, pitch, beat, or tempo. The artist's motivation determines the value of music. If the intent is improvement of the human spirit, that music deserves consideration. And if the artist's motivation is anything less, most of us are well equipped to find the "off" switch. Helping children determine which motivation is which begins in their infancy.

And maybe it's not so important how that message arrives as that it is delivered somehow.

My mother left no options. She grew up in a family tradition of concert musicians and considered music sacred. As children, we heard the classics and popular tunes with poetic lyrics. Anything else, mother considered the deluded ravings of some maniac. And, without any particular master plan, I too gave my children no choices in the beginning. They were subjected to endless piano recitals in utero, and as infants took naps on my lap at the keyboard to the strains of Beethoven, Bach, Chopin and Rachmaninoff. [The poor things probably slept because it constituted the only possible escape.] By age two or three, they held their little hands on mine while I played, getting the feel of the music. After awhile, they began to identify their own favorite songs and demand to "play" them.

Now they are older, and piano music is a comfort to them. "Play us to sleep," they say as they climb the stairs to bed. "We had a hard day." None of them is restricted from any other kind of music. But they have heard the sound of Beauty, however they came by it, and will not accept substitutes.

If we are to teach our children and promote their spiritual essence, we must look carefully at the values we hold in high regard, the messages we send them. We have no more important task in life. When we place electronic entertainment centers the size of battleships in the middle of the livingroom, and offer no guidance, these pleasure domes will become the altars on which our children's imaginations will be sacrificed. The raising of our children is not the province of the Entertainment Industry, they are not a Market Share. They are our sacred trust, spiritual beings whose educational curriculum must consist of beauty and of truth, and of values only we can give them.

From everything I have read, seen, or been told, the key to someone becoming an artist or developing a lifelong intimate connection with the Arts is that another human being took the time to introduce them, to encourage them, to hold open the door for that individual, if only enough to let in even the smallest light. Every human being, no matter how old or young, deserves that opportunity. We who understand must take the time to say, "Let me show you. Look in here and see what I love so much. For all of this also belongs to you."

Chapter Thirteen

The letter from the publisher thanked me for my book proposal saying, "Your messages are very good, and truly a pleasure to read. Unfortunately, your proposal does not fit into our focus." Doesn't fit? Why had they asked me to submit it, I wondered? I called the head of project development to inquire about this strange turn of events. And her explanation left my head spinning. This wasn't at all the proposal she had expected, wasn't the book I had described to her in our meeting. It wasn't? No, she said very definitely. I had described a book about my own artistic values, personal trials and transformation, a self-portrait; nothing to do with a biography of José Carreras, operatic star. He was mentioned in our discussions only as an inspirational catalyst, she said, and was clearly not the protagonist of the work I proposed.

How could that be? My intent had always been to write about José Carreras. That had never changed, never altered for a moment. I thanked her for her consideration of the abstract and hung up. Then, baffled, turned on the computer and flipped through the pages of the first five chapters of my manuscript. My God. It was true. I was writing about myself. Now, this took the prize. No one could unknowingly write the wrong book. More wasted time and effort. And, if Carreras accepted my project proposal, I had no publisher. What a disaster.

The second bombshell fell a week later. It had been launched from London by Mr. Carreras' agents there –

Dear Ms Warren:

Mr. Fritz Krammer, Secretary to José Carreras has forwarded a copy of your letter of February 4, and has instructed us to reply...
Unfortunately Mr. Carreras is unable to give his permission for you to proceed with your book

concept...the reason being that an agreement has already been reached and work begun on a similar book project that has Mr. Carreras' endorsement.

However, Mr. Carreras would like to thank you for your interest.

With kind regards.

I read the letter through four or five times and placed it before me on the kitchen table. Emotions crossed, mixed, collided and blurred. Once more, somebody else was writing my book!

After years of effort, just another maddening irony. That it was a very thoughtful rejection notice seemed little consolation.

No, I didn't want consolation. In fact, I would just heap up the books, the research, the video recordings, the tapes and compact discs, the computer print-outs, and the music. I would stack them out in the garden and burn them! With the rising flames I would see the end of this! The end of emotional torment, mental torture, disappointment, frustration! Yes, I screamed inside, that is how I would answer this horrible letter!

Angels! Guests! Inspiration! Where are you now? Do you hear me? I followed the path. I did what you said. And here I face another wall of thorns! You know you will burn with these dreams! You know I will too! Are you going to leave me here alone? Silence.

They wouldn't tell me the answer. They sent my daughter to comfort me instead. Rachel walked in just in time to see the first tears roll down my face. With a look of panic, she snatched up the letter and read it.

"Don't cry, Mama," she said, "They're rejecting a book you're not even writing. Your book is better anyway."

"It's not that," I explained, "It's just that after all these years... And this is the end?... Seeing it in black and white. It's just so ...final."

So final when nothing else about the night Carreras sang had ever gotten even remotely clear. So absolute when the purpose of all of it seemed nebulous. What did it mean? I still had no

170

glimmer of an explanation for the single event which had precipitated years of cataclysmic upheaval and personal change. What had I heard? How had the message, whatever it was, been transmitted? What was the form of communication? Would I ever know? And why had this happened to me of all people...a fool who cannot tolerate the thought of a random occurrence, an unanswered question?

Only once before had I encountered anything similar. And to my great frustration, that mystery had dangled, achingly unsolvable for all these years. That event also involved a strange, never-explained message I had received over the air waves. This first inexplicable message arrived in a profoundly haunting manner, and was about a dear friend, the president of our college, Dr. Robert Christie. He had taken over as President during my sophomore year and, as an editor of the university newspaper, I had served on numerous student committees he chaired. Christie was a brilliant, dynamic and extraordinarily handsome man; someone who exuded a vitality, radiance and intelligence that was evident from the moment he entered the room. He was culturally astute, conversant in several languages, knowledgeable in the Arts and the Sciences, at home in any situation. His vision of education, of the purpose of the university, made every discussion with him an inspired event, every momentary exchange a joy and a memory. He was the hero of a lifetime, a man to be intensely admired, and quoted often. I was honored to be considered among his many friends.

Just out of college and getting situated in a new apartment, I was somehow vaguely aware that Dr. Christie had planned an archaeological tour with his wife and two small children during their vacation. But, that was certainly not primary in my thoughts when, while arranging furniture in my new home, I had dropped the stereo turntable, disconnecting wires underneath. I heated up the soldering iron to attempt to fix the damage. The entire system consisted of only a turntable and two speakers and I had torn it apart and reassembled it in the past to save repair fees. This time, although repair had looked relatively hopeless, I replaced a couple wires and the turntable lurched into action once more. And, just as it did, without benefit of any radio or receiver, the sound of a foreign radio station or communication device of some sort began to broadcast through the speakers into the apartment.

The transmission was all in Spanish, a language I had just studied intensively for six years. Every word came through with crystal clarity. A light plane was down in the Mexican jungle. The man who was speaking was standing at the crash site and describing the scene. The pilot and all four passengers were dead, he said. The passengers, whom he had identified from papers they carried, were tourists: Dr. Robert Christie, his wife, his son and daughter. As quickly as the message had begun, it ended. I never before had received any transmission through a stereo turntable and could not believe it possible.

However, afraid to ignore such a compelling event, I called a friend, the Dean of Student Activities at the school, and explained what had happened and that, electronically speaking, the transmission of such a message from Mexico to Pennsylvania via a stereo turntable and speakers seemed impossible. Nonetheless, I was positive of what had been said. The Dean came over to look at the machine which had carried this incredible news and was equally confounded. Although we could confirm no reports about Dr. Christie with any radio stations or newspapers, my friend decided to notify the college trustees of what I had heard. Fortunately, they met through the night to decide on a strategy if the message proved true. The next day, news came from Mexico City: all the Christies had died in a light airplane crash in a remote jungle. From what we could determine, no one could have transmitted a message from that primitive location. And, just as strange, how could I have heard these words -- however they were delivered -- when no one else did?

I refuse to accept a ruling of "occult" or "supernatural." These terms only describe situations we do not yet have the wherewithal to explain properly. In scientific terms, "occult" really means "we don't know and, since it's not a priority, we're not sure when we'll get around to figuring it out."

We can all readily appreciate at this time in history that classic physical science offers us something rare and wonderful in the interpretation of natural phenomena. The comfort and stability of fact. The immediate and complete correspondence among symbols, words and reality. Cause and effect, action and reaction, momentum, leverage, Newton's Apple. Quantum physics presents other possibilities. More confusing, more complex, and ultimately, more wonderful; perhaps even the hope of comprehending what we now helplessly refer to as "supernatural."

For scientists candidly recognize that words, realities, and symbols do not adequately describe the subatomic world in relation to ours. Whatever we attempt to measure changes before our eyes. Particles evade and outrun us. We find ourselves short of language to describe invisible relationships. Discover that our attempts at painting concrete pictorial descriptions of particles, waves and reactions break down. We struggle to cope in a universe where light cannot escape the perimeter of the black holes in deep space so that we can ever hope to see inside.

We find that, even in the language of pure mathematics, we cannot transfer the concepts of quantum theory adequately from that realm into ours. Without "logos" to support us we are soon relying on "mythos" as our guide. As Gary Zukav explained, "A mathematical analysis of subatomic phenomena is not better qualitatively than any other symbolic analysis, because symbols do not follow the same rules as experience. They follow rules of their own. In short, the problem is not in the language, the problem is the language."

Why does language fail? Because, in discoveries which will probably constitute what Zukav calls "the End of Science" as a discipline separate from the rest of knowledge, physicists have determined that particles communicate at a speed faster than light. We have no means to describe this phenomenon. So far as we have ever known, this is impossible. The definition of every current tenet of physics depends upon the premise that nothing travels faster than light. Experiments with photons, the smallest element of illumination, have changed all that.

Assumptions were once absolute that electrons in an excited state emit photons in pairs which, because of their proximity, their locality, will cue each other on the direction of their spin. Spin photon A to the North, for example, and photon B automatically adjusts to a spin South. More recent experiments have shown that pairs of photons which are emitted into opposite and remote scientific arenas communicate without any contact with one another. They somehow "know" if their photon twin has altered its direction of spin and adjust, regardless of their locality, regardless of separations by extreme distance. Not only that, attempts to alter the spin of photon A so quickly that B cannot adjust have failed. The communication between photons happens instantaneously. Scientists cannot "trick" them.

As a result, we now recognize the existence of Superluminary Communication, a form of apparently telepathic subatomic communication that occurs at a speed exceeding that of light. Can the presence of that phenomenon, expanded into the macroscopic world explain a mental message from an event recorded ten thousand miles away; a message whose reality has no other explanation? Can it explain a clear signal from a nonexistent transmitter in the jungles of Mexico?

Had I found the communication channel for the one Truth I sought, for the essence behind the Light? Is this instantaneous connection my means of knowing my father was bleeding alone in a hospital, was drugged and wandering the hallway in need of assistance? Was this the place "below wherever roots go," where my father and I are connected? Was this the source of communication with the Angels, with the Uncle who loved me? Could this be the ether which carried the farewell of a dying man? Did all these Truths thrive in the same atmosphere as the voice of one who sings from his Soul, whose spirit had radiated its light halfway across the world?

The discovery of The End of Science offers me great hope. I long ago gave up trying to understand how I got news of Dr. Christie. It seemed for a while I must also relinquish the hope of comprehending these experiences of the past three years, because scientific and philosophic interpretations fell short of making the theoretical and verbal translation from abstract logic to visible fact. With new knowledge, all that has changed.

Even so, we must look to future developments for definitive answers. The Second Law of Thermodynamics, the Law of Entropy, assures us that the past is hardest to interpret; that from the moment an event transpires, its particle contents begin to scatter into endless space. In contrast, future events are forming ahead of us in space and time, becoming ever more certain. The present and future will be our most reliable sources of information. And that is where we must look if we are to find answers to unexplained phenomena. We can not go back.

I have read that the use of scientific theory, that holding up particle physics as the exemplification of essentially macroscopic or spiritual phenomena constitutes the ultimate triumph of materialism. I disagree. For, after all, every child wants to understand the source of a volcano's explosive power, the forces which create the ocean's waves, the substance of a cloud. And such knowledge makes these realities only more personal, more indescribably beautiful. Human curiosity exists and thrives because it propels us toward the future, toward our destiny, our spiritual home. It is part of the music, the myth, the science, the senses, the Art, which unite us. Curiosity represents our fascination with the essence of Truth behind the light.

The night after the arrival of the letter from London, I could not sleep and took the telescope outside, in search of the star system Alpha Centauri. For, among the stars, within the galaxies, black holes, supernovas and comets, human disappointments take on more realistic proportions. True, the risk had been great. I had crossed the Sea. But I had help. My family had been there from the beginning. And so many friends had joined in. An Angel, inspiration, and, of course, that incorrigible Guest. Now I stood on the opposite shore, gazing over the route of my journey. Was this the end?

"The end? Transcend!," said the Voice.

Finally. I had come to the center, the inner calm. And that is what spoke.

"Think." it said. "What have you learned? The journey goes on eternally in tempo with the universal song. There is no end, nor a beginning. Keep quiet. Listen. Do you hear it?"

I strained my ears. Held my breath. And faintly from the distance heard the familiar sound, the notes, floating on the night....my melody.

I heard. And in hearing knew that anger, disappointment, self pity would carry me nowhere. I must sing the melody. Sing with all that was in me, in my heart, soul, and mind. For only then could the other Voices find me and sing along. I must sing the tale, the book, the story. This was my melody. My birthright. My destiny. This was the gift of the journey, the Hero Journey described by Campbell's universal monomyth. Typically, it all begins with the Herald, he said, calling us to adventure and to a state of roiling internal crisis.

Our first serious encounter is with the protective figure -- the Angel -- who offers supernatural aid. Then, with great trepidation, grasping our sense of magnified power, we plunge across the threshold into the unknown, descend into the belly of the whale, into the realm of trials, uncertainty, doubts, and fear. We search everywhere for the prize of unity with ourselves, with our kind, with every kind. And, riding the wings of that unity, come to the state of apotheosis, of calm, of a silent center. Finally, wrestling within our deepest consciousness, we break through our personal limitations: defensiveness, doubt, egotism, prejudice, ignorance. And, if we are sincere, discover the font of life, our own inner core.

Now the difficult task remains. To return with the life-transforming trophy. The answer. To step back into the real world and, unfettered, without apology, to translate the experience, to share the gifts given along the way. I felt unequal to such a task. That was the real barrier of thorns. How would I condense this incredible experience into mere words? It seemed impossible. Science and philosophy offered all the excuses: words are inadequate, they said. Yet I must translate somehow. Or I would feel forever doomed to loneliness, to solitary confinement with this inspiration.

Collapsing the telescope, I returned to the house and stood before the bookcase. Somewhere, there was a poem. A poem about a singer. Was it Whitman? Yes, Whitman. I pulled the book from the shelf and opened to a spot where I thought I had seen it. "The Mystic Trumpeter," it said at the top of the page. No. That wasn't it. The one I had wanted was about a tenor. But, just the same, I began reading --

1.

"Hark, some wild trumpeter, some strange musician,
Hovering unseen in air, vibrates capricious tunes tonight.

I hear thee trumpeter, listening alert I catch thy notes,
Now pouring, whirling like a tempest round me.
Now low, subdued, now in the distance lost.

2.

Come nearer bodiless one, haply in thee resounds
Some dead composer, haply thy pensive life
'Was fill'd with aspirations high, unform'd ideals,
Waves, oceans musical, chaotically surging,
That now ecstatic ghost, close to me bending, thy cornet echoing, pealing
Gives out to no one's ears but mine, but freely give to mine
That I may thee translate.

3.

Blow trumpeter free and clear, I follow thee,
While at thy liquid prelude, glad, serene,
The fretting world, the streets, the noisy hours of day withdraw
A holy calm descends like dew upon me,
I walk in cool refreshing night the walks of Paradise,
I scent the grass, the moist air and the roses;
Thy song expands my numb'd imbonded spirit, thou freest, launchest me,
Floating and basking upon heaven's lake.

7.

Oh trumpeter, methinks I am myself the instrument thou playest,
Thou melt'st my heart, my brain --thou movest, drawest, changest them at will;
And now thy sullen notes send darkness through me,

Thou takest away all cheering light, all hope,
I see the enslaved, the overthrown, the hurt, the opprest of the
    whole earth,
I feel the measureless shame and humiliation of my race, it
    becomes all mine,
Mine too the revenges of humanity, the wrongs of ages, baffled
    feuds and hatreds,
Utter defeat upon me weighs--all lost--the foe victorious,
(Yet, 'mid the ruins Pride colossal stands unshaken to the last,
Endurance, resolution to the last.)

8.

Now trumpeter for thy close,
Vouchsafe a higher strain than any yet,
Sing to my soul, renew its languishing faith and hope,
Rouse up my slow belief, give me some vision of the future,
Give me for once its prophecy and joy.

O glad, exulting, culminating song!
A vigor more than earth's is in thy notes,
Marches of victory -- man disenthral'd -- the conqueror at last,
Hymns to the universal God from universal man -- all joy!

A reborn race appears -- a perfect world, all joy !
Women and men in wisdom innocence and health -- all joy!
Riotous laughing bacchanals fill'd with joy!
War, sorrow, suffering gone -- the rank earth purged -- nothing but
joy left!
The ocean fill'd with joy -- the atmosphere with joy!
Joy! Joy! in freedom, worship, love! joy in the ecstasy of life.
Enough to merely be! Enough to breathe!
Joy! Joy! all over joy!

Whitman had heard the Herald too! He had known the
exultation, intrigue and fear that accompanied the Herald's
appearance. He would have understood, if I had explained the
night Carreras sang; the night the Herald spoke. Someone else,
this magnificent poet, had stood in my place, had returned from
the Journey and gloriously transformed his inspirational dilemma
into poetry, into song.

Perhaps salvation was in simply attempting the same. In finishing the Book I knew how to write. In telling the story of the Plunge to the Sea, The Guest, the Music and the Angels. Perhaps, redemption was in becoming the Herald for others. In reaching out to those who breathed the breath of mere survival, whose spirits longed to create but who lived in confusion and numbness, disconnected from their strength, outside themselves; not dead, just buried alive. As I had lived only one short year ago.

If I could, I would give away many times over the gift given to me. I would sing out over the air waves to those who suffer this torment, alone and afraid, "Listen to my voice! Hear the echo of the melody inside you. Today the Journey begins. Awaken the Hero within! The Angels, the Music await you. It is not too late."

Please, give me a sign, God, I cried. Is that the message? Did I get it right? Until I know for certain, Whitman will be the North Star. I will trust his example, and that of the new, the latest Visitor. He arrived one night last week, apparently drawn by the Chopin "Nocturne" I played on the piano. And, taking up residence on the garden wall, he commenced a concerto of trills, cadenzas and grace notes that would break the stoniest heart.

"What is it?," the children said in unison, and ran to peer into the darkness, to catch a glimpse of this remarkable bird. Even before Rachel announced his identity, I knew what bird this must be.

"I see him!," she said. "It's a nightingale! Where does somebody so small get such a powerful voice?"

We had never heard a nightingale here, only in aviaries in Philadelphia. I didn't know they could survive the extremes of the desert. Yet, there he sat, trilling away. Now he arrives every night, after dark, to sing a lilting duet with the piano. Hearing him, I am once more determined. His songs are the sounds, the living proof, of our world of Beauty and Harmony creating and renewing itself. In the midst of such faith, I will not relinquish my dreams. And, one day, I will come face to face with the source of my inspiration, with the only one who can answer the remaining questions.

Meanwhile, there is joyful, hopeful work to be done. For, if God's messenger, this lovely nightingale, so delicate, ephemeral, shy and vulnerable can sing from his soul in the darkness of night, all who hear and comprehend must accompany him. It is his birthright and our destiny to proclaim the eternal melody.

ABOUT THE AUTHOR....

Nancy Warren, author of "Hello, Mr. Carreras," was born in Philadelphia and raised in northern Bucks County, Pennsylvania. She was educated at the University of Pennsylvania in creative writing, Spanish literature and journalism, and is a member of Pi Delta Epsilon Honorary National Journalism Fraternity.

In her early career, she worked in public relations and charity fundraising, in Spanish language translation, and as a fashion model. She later held executive positions in the development of a conglomerate corporation, including a delinquency treatment program, a video production company, and a chain of retail clothing boutiques. She also served on several corporate boards of directors and as a corporate trouble shooter. Nancy co-authored a book to do with the habilitation of juvenile delinquents in the United States and has published magazine articles and poetry. As an amateur, she performed vocal and classical piano music.

The author's career direction changed dramatically when she happened to hear Mr. José Carreras singing and, as a result, enacted a lifelong dream to undertake a career in classical music. She became Assistant Stage Director at Arizona Opera Company in 1992, Production Stage Manager in 1994 and the Company's Production Director in 1995.

She was production chief for the Arizona Opera Company's flagship effort -- two consecutive cycles of the Wagnerian Ring -- performed in 1996 and 1998, under the executive direction of impressario, Glynn Ross, reknowned as creator of the first Wagnerian Ring Festival in the United States.

Printed in the United States
3383